SERIES EDITOR: LEE JOHNS

LOUIS XV's ARMY (5)
COLONIAL & NAVAL TROOPS

WRITTEN BY
RENÉ CHARTRAND

PLATES BY
EUGÈNE LELIÈPVRE

OSPREY
MILITARY

First published in Great Britain in 1997 by Osprey, a division of
Reed Consumer Books, Michelin House, 81 Fulham Road, London SW3 6RB,
Auckland and Melbourne.

Osprey
Michelin House, 81 Fulham Road, London SW3 6RB

ISBN 1 85532 709 0

Filmset in Singapore by Pica Ltd
Printed through World Print Ltd., Hong Kong

Editor: Sharon van der Merwe
Design: Alan Hamp @ Design for Books

For a catalogue of all titles published by Osprey Military, please write to:-
Osprey Marketing, Reed Consumer Books, Michelin House,
81 Fulham Road, London SW3 6RB

Author's note

This fifth and final volume of a series devoted to the organisation,
uniforms and weapons of Louis XV's Army examines a topic
generally neglected by French metropolitan historians: the colonial
troops and militias in New France, the West Indies, Africa and India,
as well as marines and other naval troops based in France. It
completes this collection of volumes which should form the most
extensive account yet published on the organisation and material
culture of all the various types of troops that made up
Louis XV's Army.

Acknowledgments

Francis Back, Montreal; Sandy Balcom of Fortress Louisbourg;
Giancarlo Boeri, Rome; Russel Bouchard, Chicoutimi (Canada);
Jean Boudriot, Paris; Raoul Brunon of the Musée de l'Armée at
Aix-en-Provence; Gustave Gras, Paris; André Gousse of the
Canadian National Historic Sites; Albert W. Haarmann, Washington;
Peter Harrington of the Anne S.K. Brown Military Collection at
Brown University; Bruno Hélias, Plomelin (France); Arwed Ulrich
Koch, Edewecht (Germany); Eugène Lelièpvre, Montrouge (France);
Michel Pétard, Nantes.

Publisher's note

Readers may wish to study this title in conjunction with the
following Osprey publications:

Artist's note

Readers may care to note that the original paintings from which the
colour plates in this book were prepared are available for private
sale. All reproduction copyright whatsoever is retained by the
publisher. All enquiries should be addressed to:

Eugène Lelièpvre, 33 rue Boileau, 92120 Montrouge, France

The publishers regret that they can enter into no correspondence
upon this matter.

LOUIS XV'S ARMY (5)
COLONIAL & NAVAL TROOPS

INTRODUCTION

King Louis XV in his full ceremonial robes by the studio of L.M. Van Loo, c.1762. This was the king's official portrait in the later part of his reign. It was reproduced in various sizes and hung in government halls and official residences throughout the realm. This particular example hung in Port-au-Prince, Haiti, until 1797 when it was taken to Britain by General Simcoe. It came to Canada in the 1920s, along with many outstanding documents, thanks to the generosity of Lord Northcliffe. (National Archives of Canada, C604)

In 1715, when the infant Louis XV became king, France had a sizeable overseas empire in America, Africa and Asia. The colonies in America were under the direct responsibility of the royal government and were administered through the Ministry of the Navy. In North America, there was the vast expanse of New France which included Ile Royale and its tributary Ile St Jean (now Cape Breton Island and Prince Edward Island) at the entrance of the St Lawrence River. The Fortress of Louisbourg was built on Ile Royale from the 1720s. Canada consisted of the St Lawrence River valley with the cities of Quebec, (the capital of New France) Trois-Rivières and Montreal, and extended westward to the western prairies. Louisiana, the newest colony in New France, stretched from Alabama to Texas and up the Mississippi River to the south of the Great Lakes. Its main centres were Mobile and New Orleans, the capital, and Fort de Chartres in Illinois. New France thus formed an immense arc around the British seaboard colonies and was interconnected by a string of forts in the wilderness. But its population was very small compared to that of its British neighbour.

In the West Indies, Saint-Domingue (Haiti) was the largest and richest of the French colonies and it was divided into three districts: the northern with its capital Le Cap (Cap-Haitien) was the most prosperous, the western with Port-au-Prince as capital and the southern with Saint-Louis. From 1714, Haiti had its own governor-general. The other governor-general ruled the French Leeward islands from Martinique. French Guyana was then a small settlement consisting mainly of the town of Cayenne with a few outposts in the interior.

Colonies in Africa and Asia (and Louisiana for a short time) were ruled as concessions by the king to the *Compagnie des Indes*, or French East India Company, the equivalent and competitor of the British Honourable East India Company. It had a ruling council in Paris, a naval base and troop depot at Lorient, forts on the coast of Senegal, and outposts in Guinea. In the Indian Ocean were the islands of Ile de France (Mauritius) and Ile de Bourbon (La Réunion). In India, Pondichery (south of Madras) was the capital of French India. Relatively modest until the late 1730s, French India expanded considerably into central India until the Seven Years' War.

Lack of comprehensive support, policy and strategy by the French government doomed the vast empires of New France and India which were abandoned, save for a few outposts, by the 1763 Treaty of Paris. However, France retained a sizeable number of colonies, including Haiti which became the world's most prosperous colony.

These colonies were garrisoned by thousands of regular officers and soldiers who belonged to the Navy's colonial establishment or by the French East India Company's troops. This represented some 4,500 European officers and men in 1720; about 6,500 Europeans with some 5,000 Sepoys in 1740; 13,000 Europeans with about 10,000 Sepoys in 1756; and about 8,800 Europeans and 1,000 Sepoys by 1770. The Navy had its own establishment of troops based in France for sea service, hovering between 6,000 and 11,000 officers and men. These troops did not form part of the regular army seen in the previous volumes, and are not usually covered in histories of the French forces. Yet, since the end of the 17th century, they saw most action against the enemy overseas (usually the British) and in ships on the high seas; it was only from 1755 that metropolitan army battalions first saw action overseas. Thus, we are dealing with a largely 'unknown' colonial and naval army. Much of the information given below is entirely new and abstracted from considerable historical data.

Melchior Jordy de Cabagnac, officer in the Canadian Compagnies franches de la Marine, c.1720. Before the 1730s, officers in Canada often had no uniforms. A red coat with gold lace and buttons, such as shown on this portrait, seemed to have been a popular choice. Although no one actually wore a cuirass, it was shown in the portrait to indicate the military status of the sitter. Jordy de Cabagnac was born in Canada in 1695, commissioned in 1715 and served with distinction until his death in 1763. He was knighted in 1758 and the cross of the Military Order of Saint Louis hanging on a scarlet ribbon was later added on the painting. (National Archives of Canada, C10540)

COLONIAL REGULAR TROOPS

Colonial Compagnies franches de la Marine

As the colonies in America were administered by the Ministry of the Navy, the troops in various colonies were raised, paid, clothed and regulated by that ministry. Organised as independent companies, each colony had its own military establishment. The enlistment period was to be six years, but troops could be retained for longer if the governor felt he was short of men. In Canada and Louisiana, the soldiers were encouraged to become settlers when their service was over and thousands did so. Many officers also settled in Canada, and officer's commissions tended to be granted to their sons who were admitted as cadets. This was especially common in Canada where, by the 1750s, nearly all colonial officers were born in the country. By contrast, all new recruits serving in the ranks came from France.

New France: Canada

The first three companies arrived in Quebec in November 1683. From 1699, there were 28 companies each having 30 men led by three officers; from 1722, four officers led 29 men, a number further reduced to 28 enlisted men on 8 May 1731 when a *Cadet à l'aiguillette* (gentleman cadet) was added to each company. In May 1749, the establishment was raised to 50 men, and the number of companies augmented to 30 in April 1750. A drum-major and a fifer were officially added, but had actually existed since the late 17th century. The number of men was raised to 65 per company in March 1756 and the number of companies raised to 40 in March 1757, but there were already some 250 men missing to complete the establishment. In July 1757 500 soldiers were organised into an eight-company battalion to serve with Montcalm's metropolitan troops (see MAA 302 *Louis XV's Army Vol. 2*). In early 1760 a second battalion was added, as well as a company of grenadiers for each battalion.

This battalion was often termed 'Régiment de la Marine' by French metropolitan officers in their memoirs, which has confused some historians. In fact, it had nothing to do with the senior metropolitan infantry regiment.

Most Canadian companies (19 out of 28 in the 1740s) were based in Montreal, but many of their officers and men were detached in outlying forts and outposts as far away as present-day Saskatchewan. They were the only regular infantry in Canada until 1755, and took part in just about every battle from the end of the 17th century until the surrender of Montreal on 8 September 1760. The remnants were sent to France and incorporated into the eight army battalions that had served in Canada on 25 December 1760.

Ile Royale (Louisbourg)

In 1714, the former garrisons of Acadia and Placentia, Newfoundland, were united into an establishment of seven companies of Ile Royale Compagnies franches de la Marine, each having three officers and 50 men. Reduced to six companies in 1722, each company was augmented by an officer and ten men in 1723, and formed eight companies from March 1730. There were two *Cadets à l'aiguillette* and 58 men per company from June 1732, and each company was raised to 68 men, two cadets and four officers from May 1741.

They participated in the capture of Canso, Nova Scotia, in 1744, and the siege and surrender of fortress Louisbourg in May and June 1745. Companies evacuated to Rochefort (France) were sent back to reinforce the garrison of Quebec in 1747-1749. The companies were sent back to Louisbourg in 1749, following the return of the fortress to France in 1748. In March 1749, the garrison was augmented to 24 companies of four officers and 50 men each, including two cadets. A drum-major and a fifer were also added.

The Ile Royale companies were nearly all posted at Louisbourg, only a few being detached to Port Toulouse, Port Dauphin and usually a company at Ile Saint-Jean (today Prince Edward Island). Discipline, which had been somewhat lax in the early 1740s, was considerably improved from 1751 and these troops served bravely during the very hard siege of 1758 against overwhelming odds. Transferred to Rochefort, 400 of its men in eight companies were with the few doomed ships sent to Canada which ended up battling the British in the Restigouche River in July 1760. About half escaped back to France. On 25 December 1760, the Ile Royale troops were incorporated into the eight army battalions that had served in New France.

Charles Le Moyne, second Baron de Longueuil (1687-1755), wearing the uniform of the Compagnies franches de la Marine in Canada, c.1733. Note the white sleeve and blue cuff with three gold buttons. The barony de Longueuil was created by Louis XIV to reward the Le Moyne family for its outstanding service. The second baron saw much service on the staff in Montreal or leading expeditions deep into the wilderness, including the Canadian contingent sent to fight the Chickasaw Indians in Louisiana during 1739-1740. (Musée d'art, Joliette, Quebec)

Louisiana

The first two Louisiana Compagnies franches de la Marine were created in 1703. Augmented to four companies in 1714, there were eight in 1716, each with three officers and 50 enlisted men. On 23 August 1717, these troops were transferred to the Occidental and later the French East India Company until 1731 when the colony reverted to the royal domain and the eight companies became royal colonial troops again. In November 1732, the Louisiana Compagnies franches de la Marine grew to 13 companies each having four officers and 50 men. In 1738, a *Cadet à l'aiguillette* was added, while the number of men was reduced to 49. In September 1750, the garrison was nearly tripled to 37 companies, which were reduced to 36 in 1754 and 35 in November 1759. Following the cession of Louisiana to Spain and Britain in 1763, the much depleted 35 companies were reduced to six which remained until disbanded when Spanish troops arrived in 1769.

The Louisiana Compagnies franches de la Marine were posted mostly in New Orleans, Mobile and at Fort de Chartres in Illinois, with small detachments scattered in forts along the Mississippi and Missouri rivers as well as northern Alabama. They often served against hostile Indians, especially the Chikasaws, but were allied with the Cherokees. During the Seven Years' War, numerous Louisiana troops were sent to the Ohio Valley where they fought with distinction.

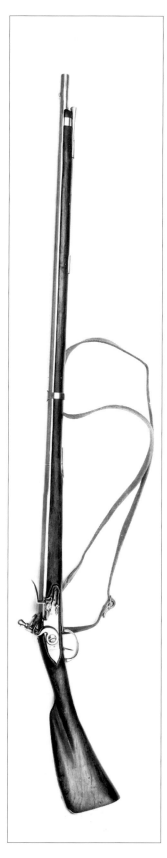

West Indies and Guyana:

Martinique and the Leeward Islands: The first colonial Compagnies franches de la Marine to be raised and sent overseas arrived at Martinique in late 1674 and were dispersed to other French islands. In 1714, the establishment was split in two, that of Saint-Domingue and that of 'Isle du Vent' (Martinique and the other Leeward Islands). There were then 14 companies assigned to the Leewards, each having three officers and 50 enlisted men. They were reduced to ten companies in 1724 following the arrival in Martinique of a company of the Karrer (Swiss) Regiment. The garrison doubled to 20 companies from October 1750. Most companies were stationed in Martinique, with the rest on Guadeloupe, Grenada and St Lucia. They were quiet garrisons until January 1759 when the troops in Martinique repulsed a British attack on Fort Royal, but Guadeloupe fell in May. Martinique was attacked again and surrendered to the British in February 1762, followed by St Lucia and Grenada in March. The companies were transferred to Rochefort and disbanded on 25 March 1763.

Saint-Domingue (Haiti): When made a distinct establishment in 1714, there were 12 companies, each having two officers and 50 enlisted men. They were reduced to eight companies from October 1721 when a

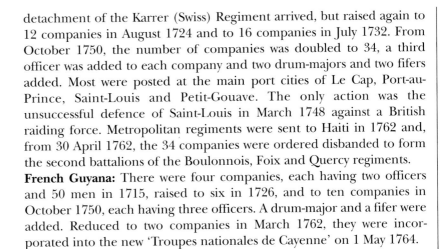

FAR LEFT **Bayonet for the Tulle naval infantry musket with its distinctive long branch. This rather old-fashioned type of bayonet was carried until the early 1750s. This example was found at Fort Beauséjour National Historic Site, a site garrisoned by the Compagnies franche from 1751 to 1755.**

LEFT **Naval infantry musket. Reproduction based on the contract of 1734 between the Navy and the arms factories at Tulle. (Fortress Louisbourg National Historic Site, Louisbourg, Nova Scotia)**

Cartridge box wooden block with nine holes and with its leather casing for the *gargoussier*-style box. This exceptional artefact was found at Fortress Louisbourg. (Fortress Louisbourg National Historic Site, Louisbourg, Nova Scotia)

detachment of the Karrer (Swiss) Regiment arrived, but raised again to 12 companies in August 1724 and to 16 companies in July 1732. From October 1750, the number of companies was doubled to 34, a third officer was added to each company and two drum-majors and two fifers added. Most were posted at the main port cities of Le Cap, Port-au-Prince, Saint-Louis and Petit-Gouave. The only action was the unsuccessful defence of Saint-Louis in March 1748 against a British raiding force. Metropolitan regiments were sent to Haiti in 1762 and, from 30 April 1762, the 34 companies were ordered disbanded to form the second battalions of the Boulonnois, Foix and Quercy regiments.

French Guyana: There were four companies, each having two officers and 50 men in 1715, raised to six in 1726, and to ten companies in October 1750, each having three officers. A drum-major and a fifer were added. Reduced to two companies in March 1762, they were incorporated into the new 'Troupes nationales de Cayenne' on 1 May 1764.

UNIFORMS, ARMS AND ACCOUTREMENTS

From 1716, the issue uniform was basically the same for all soldiers, be they in the colonies or serving as marines. On 17 January, the Navy Council ruled that 'with regards to the clothing of the [Navy's] colonial troops, it is intended that...in the future, they will be dressed as those of the Navy [marines based in France] for the sergeants as well as for the soldiers and drummers'. The new uniform for all troops in France and America was a grey-white coat with blue cuffs and lining, blue waistcoat, breeches and stockings, white cravat, and a hat edged with false gold lace. There were three dozen large brass buttons and three dozen small brass buttons per waistcoat. In the year of the 'great clothing' issue, each enlisted man in every company received a coat which was to last two years, with breeches, pairs of stockings, pairs of shoes, shirts, and a hat. The next year was the 'small clothing' issue, when a waistcoat, to last two years, was provided, along with all the other items of yearly issue.[1]

The coat, originally very ample, was becoming more fitted by 1740 so that less cloth was needed to make it. Coat pockets each had five buttons from c.1716, but this was reduced to three in c.1740. There were usually three buttons per coat cuff. From 1743, white gaiters were issued. It is important to note that the coats of the colonial Compagnies franches had no collars (Plate A).

Sergeants had the same uniform made of better materials, with gilt buttons and gold hat lace. From 1716 to 1749, they wore gold laces at the cuffs' buttonholes as rank badges. Thereafter, sergeants had gold lace edging the cuffs and pocket flaps, sergeant-majors having two laces.

---

1 In the West Indies and Guyana, the blue waistcoat was initially replaced in 1716 by a grey-white linen 'coat' with 18 brass buttons with a 'small clothing' issue of grey-white linen breeches and stockings every second year. But this proved unsuitable and blue waistcoats, breeches and stockings were issued from the early 1720s.

Sergeant's halberd heads found at Louisbourg. The one at the centre is of the older style with the axe blade. (Fortress Louisbourg National Historic Site, Louisbourg, Nova Scotia)

Drummers and fifers wore the blue coat with red cuffs and lining of the king's livery, red waistcoat, breeches and stockings, brass buttons, and false gold hat lace. The drummers' coats were trimmed with the 'small' livery lace. Those of drum-majors had the 'grand' livery lace with gold buttons and hat lace. Up to 1730, blue waistcoats, breeches and stockings were sometimes sent instead of the regulation red. Thereafter, these items were always red.

The *Cadets à l'aiguillette* had the same weapons, equipment and uniform as private soldiers. They were distinguished by an aiguillette, as their name indicates, which was of blue and white silk with brass tips and worn on the right shoulder.

Officers were supposed to wear uniforms but often did not. The problem seems to have been one of supply. In 1731, material to make officers' uniforms was sent to Canada. This measure was successful and other colonies followed suit.

Officers and men in Canada and upper Louisiana also had a peculiar costume besides the issue uniform (Plate D). Officers soon discovered that Canadian militiamen were ideally dressed for expeditions which took them hundreds of kilometres deep into the wilderness in canoes and on foot. The officers and soldiers on such campaigns adopted the same dress, which usually consisted of a cap and a *capot,* which was a naval hooded cloth coat fastened by a sash at the waist. The garments below the waist were Indian: the breechclout was a piece of rectangular cloth which went between the legs and slipped over a waistbelt; the *mitasses* were long leggings of cloth or soft leather; moccasins were soft leather shoes without heels. It seems that the uniform waistcoats were sometimes used in summer instead of the capot.

The European style uniform was initially sent on to distant small western forts in North America. When Gilles Hocquart became Intendant in 1731, he put a stop to this expensive practice. In future, soldiers would leave Montreal in their regulation uniform but would get replacement clothing from the fort's trade store. From various bits of evidence, it seems the soldiers in such outposts kept their European style uniform for more formal occasions and wore capots for ordinary duties.

The military muskets supplied to the French Navy came from the arms manufacturer at Tulle. They had a calibre of 16.7 mm. The wooden stock had furnishings of polished iron and a wooden ramrod. The barrel, which was initially fastened to the stock by pins, was 113 cm in 1716, then lengthened to 119 cm from 1729. The reddish brown sling was held by a 'turning' ring screwed into the stock behind the counter lock plate on one end, and to a ring fixed to an iron band around the middle of the barrel. From 1743, Tulle muskets were made with iron barrel bands. This rendered the Tulle Marine musket almost identical to the Army's 1728 musket and, from the 1740s, the Navy increasingly purchased Army muskets at St Etienne.

The socket bayonets made for the Tulle muskets were of a relatively archaic design. As late as 1734, they had a very long branch of about 108 mm, with a triangular and gutted blade about 243 mm long. Conventional bayonets arrived with Army muskets during the 1740s.

The soldiers' swords were the same as in the metropolitan infantry. All privates and corporals were equipped with a waistbelt of buff leather, a powder horn with brass fittings held by a narrow buff belt slung over the left shoulder, and the *gargousssier*, a ventral cartridge box worn on the waistbelt holding nine cartridges. The cartridge box was covered by a flap of reddish brown leather. From the beginning of Louis XV's reign, it had a white anchor at the centre and a white leather saw-tooth border. However, some of black leather were sent to Louisbourg in 1744. Shortly thereafter, a new reddish brown flap was supplied bearing the king's coat of arms stamped at the centre. This type of cartridge box was still in use at the beginning of the Seven Years' War.

The arrival of army battalions in New France influenced the equipment of colonial troops. During 1757, the Compagnies franches in Louisbourg adopted *gibernes* that had arrived with the two army battalions, and these were also used in Canada at about the same time (Plate D).

Halberds were carried by sergeants and spontoons by officers. When on expeditions in the wilds of Canada, the polearms were left behind.

The company of the **Cadets de Rochefort** was a military school established at Rochefort in May 1730 to train gentlemen-cadets for commissions as officers in the colonial Compagnies franches de la Marine serving in the West Indies and Guyana. There were 30 cadets, which grew to 50 from October 1750. About half were from the West Indies. Their uniform consisted of a grey-white coat and cuffs, with blue linings, waistcoats, breeches and stockings, gold buttons and gold hat lace. White plume edged the hat and black cockade was added in 1740. Drummers wore the king's livery with the grand livery lace. Dissolved in November 1761, its officers and remaining cadets were ordered incorporated into the troops in Haiti.

Raised from December 1719, **Karrer, 1752 Hallwyl (Swiss) Regiment** was transferred to the Ministry of the Navy in 1721 to supply colonial garrisons. The Colonel's company acted as a depot at Rochefort. Each company had 200 men except for the Colonel's which had at least a hundred more. Most men appear to have been German speaking. From 1722, Martinique and Haiti each had a company; a fourth company was raised and posted in Louisiana from 1732, and a fifth company was raised and sent to Haiti in 1752. From 1722 to 1745, a detachment, initially of 50 men, from the Colonel's company was posted to the Fortress of Louisbourg; this grew to 100 men in 1724, 150 from December 1741, and surrendered in 1745. In 1752, the regiment changed colonels and was henceforth named Hallwyl. The company in Martinique surrendered in February 1762. Companies remaining in Haiti and Louisiana were repatriated following the regiment's disbandment, ordered on 1 June 1763.

The uniform was a red coat, with blue cuffs, lining, waistcoat, breeches and stockings, pewter buttons, white buttonhole lace on waistcoat, silver hat lace. From c.1735, waistcoats had vertical pockets, and two rows of buttons con-

Brass button of the Compagnies franches de la Marine, c.1716-1763. (Fortress Louisbourg National Historic Site, Louisbourg, Nova Scotia)

Soldier's shoe of the colonial Compagnies franches de la Marine, part of a shipment intended for Canada which went down in the frigate *Le Machault* in 1760. (Battle of the Restigouche National Historic Site, Restigouche, Quebec)

nected by white lace, and stockings were white (Plate F). From 1761-1763, white buttonhole lace was apparently worn on the coat as well as waistcoat (this was probably not implemented for companies in Louisiana and the West Indies). Drummers wore Karrer livery: a blue coat, yellow collar, cuffs, lining, waistcoat and breeches, pewter buttons, red-yellow-blue-white livery lace, silver hat lace. Hallwyl's livery is unknown.

COLONIAL ARTILLERY CORPS

From the mid-17th century, individual master gunners, also called *Commissaires de l'artillerie* were posted in the colonies with a few assistants to oversee artillery matters and provide training. Gunnery schools were eventually established to provide trained artillerymen. The first was organised in 1697 at Quebec City where a soldier from each of the colony's 28 companies was detached to be trained as the master gunner in what soon became known as an unofficial artillery company. Similar schools were organised at Fortress Louisbourg in 1735, Mobile in Louisiana in 1744, Martinique in 1746 and Haiti had several from 1755.

On 20 June 1743, the king signed an ordinance creating a company of *canonniers-bombardiers* to serve at the Fortress of Louisbourg. Other companies were soon ordered raised elsewhere: Haiti on 19 December

Commission given by the governor of Louisiana, Louis de Kerlérec, to Cherokee Chief Okana-Stoté dated at New Orleans, 27 February 1761. Intended to impress and rally the leaders of allied Indian nations, these commissions were quite ornate. The full coat of arms of France is above the arms of Louisiana and those of the governor who is pictured centre with the chief. Kerlérec, a naval officer, wears a blue coat with red cuffs and lining, gold buttons and lace, red waistcoat laced gold, blue breeches, white stockings, and a gold-laced hat with white plume border. He holds a fan in his left hand. (United States National Archives)

1745, Martinique and the Leewards on 30 April 1747, and Canada on 10 April 1750. On 15 March 1757, a second company was ordered raised in Canada, another at Martinique on 20 November 1757 and a second company for Louisbourg on 1 February 1758. On 1 November 1759, a company was ordered raised in Louisiana. In general, a company would have about 50 men, many of whom would be detached elsewhere. For instance, gunners from Martinique were detached to Guadeloupe, Grenada, St Lucia and Marie-Galante.

All companies generally had the same conditions, pay, uniforms, equipment and weapons. Those in Canada, Louisbourg, Martinique and the Leewards fought with distinction against much stronger British forces. The companies in Louisbourg ceased to exist following the fall of the fortress in 1758, those in Canada in 1760 and those of Martinique in 1762. The company in Louisiana was disbanded in 1763 and, in March 1764, the last two companies in Haiti were ordered disbanded.

The uniform (Plate C) worn by all companies was similar: a blue coat with red cuffs, lining, waistcoat, breeches and stockings, pewter buttons, false silver hat lace, white cravat, shirt, shoes and a blue undress *surtout* (overall) with 18 pewter buttons. Corporals and privates had scarlet cloth instead of red, silver buttons and hat lace; corporals' cuffs were edged with silver lace, with two silver laces for sergeants. Officers wore the same as the men, but their uniforms were made of finer materials, and worn with a gilt gorget when on duty. Drummers wore the king's livery with the 'small' livery lace, pewter buttons and false silver hat lace. The sleeves or cuffs of their undress *surtout* had livery lace. The drums were probably the same as those of the Compagnies franches.

The belts were buff, and from 1743 onwards the men wore a *giberne* type cartridge box holding 19 rounds, slung by its own buff shoulder belt, and covered with a reddish brown leather flap stamped with the royal arms over two crossed anchors highlighted by a silver wash. They also had a leather powder flask and a priming powder flask. Their sabres had double-branched brass guards with red, white and blue sabre knots. Muskets had brass furnishings and reddish brown slings.

Following the Seven Years' War, artillery duties in the colonies were taken up by detachments of the metropolitan Royal-Artillerie, an arrangement which soon proved unsatisfactory. With the vast colonisation plans for French Guyana in 1764, came orders to raise two companies of colonial *canonniers-bombardiers* on 1 August, reduced to one company on 1 October 1765. Another colonial company of *canonniers-bombardiers* was ordered raised to serve in Mauritius on 1 December 1766 and was joined by a second company on 1 August 1768. In Haiti, two companies were ordered raised on 1 December 1768, and joined by a

Officer bearing the colonel's colour, Karrer (Swiss) Regiment, c.1725. He wears a red coat, blue cuffs, lining, waistcoat, breeches and stockings, silver buttons, silver lace on waistcoat, hat laced with silver and its brim edged with white plumes. The colour is all white with gold fleurs-de-lis and letters. (Print after watercolour)

third company from April 1771. Finally, three companies were raised from December 1774 for Martinique and the Leewards.

From 1764, the companies in Guyana wore blue coats, waistcoats and breeches, red collars, cuffs and lapels edged with white lace, red lining, silver buttons, hats edged with white, white gaiters and stockings. On 1 October 1765, the white lace edging the facings was abolished and the waistcoat and breeches were henceforth to be red. On 1 June 1767, the 'king desiring to establish uniformity in the clothing of the companies of Canonniers-Bombardiers in his colonies' ordered those in Guyana to wear blue coats lined with blue, red collars, cuffs and lapels, blue waistcoats, white breeches, brass buttons, and hats edged with yellow lace. The breeches were altered to blue in 1770. However, true uniformity was achieved in Haiti, from 1768, and Martinique from 1774, whose artillery companies wore blue coats with red collar, cuffs and lining, white waistcoats and breeches, brass buttons, yellow hat lace, and yellow epaulettes.

These gunners served the distinctive cannon made for the Navy. Nearly all were of iron, and were generally guns that were considered too worn for shipboard use, but were thought equal to be mounted in coastal fortifications. Some were new naval guns that were deemed too heavy for ships. There were also occasional shipments of new naval guns of ship's weight. The cannon were black mounted on red naval carriages with black ironwork. Large calibre iron mortars were also found in major forts in all colonies. The lower calibre guns, of iron or brass, on field carriages were very few.

Besides the colonial gunners were a number of specialist companies. In 1757, a company of *ouvriers* (artisans) was raised locally among Canadian settlers and served with the colonial artillery until the surrender of the French forces. After the Seven Years' War, a company of *ouvriers* and a company of miners for service in Guyana were ordered raised on 1 August 1764, but were disbanded on 1 October 1765 and possibly never actually formed. A company of *ouvriers* for Mauritius was ordered raised on 1 August 1767, and joined by a second company in March 1769. Meanwhile, two companies were created for Haiti on 20 March 1768. These artisan companies were not deemed too useful; all were disbanded and the men incorporated into the new colonial infantry regiments from August 1772.

The uniform, if any, of the Canadian *ouvriers* is unknown. The companies in Mauritius and Haiti had blue coats with black collar, cuffs and lapels, pewter buttons, white buttonhole lace, white waistcoats and breeches, and black cravats. The Mauritius companies had a helmet of black boiled leather with a brass plate and a black mane. The Haiti companies wore hats edged with white lace.

Drummers in artillery and *ouvriers*' companies all wore the king's livery with the small livery lace. The drums were probably of brass with blue wooden hoops from the 1760s.

Officers had the same uniform as their men, but of superior quality cloth trimmed with gold or silver lace depending on the button colour.

Fusilier, Hallwyl (Swiss) Regiment, c.1763. Red coat, blue collar, cuffs, lining, waistcoat and breeches, white lace and pewter buttons. (Print after Marbot)

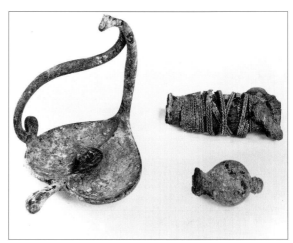

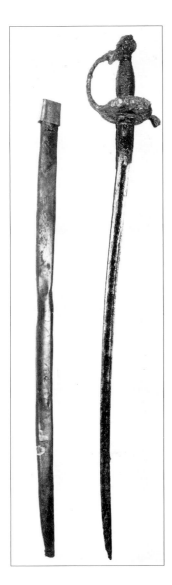

Sabre and scabbard of the *canonniers-bombardiers* posted at Fortress Louisbourg between 1743 and 1758. The mountings are of brass and only a branch is missing. (Fortress Louisbourg National Historic Site, Louisbourg, Nova Scotia)

LEFT Guard pieces of a sabre of the *canonniers-bombardiers*, c.1743-1758. The guard is complete with its ornate curving second branch. The grip was of wood with wire wrapped over it. (Fortress Louisbourg National Historic Site, Louisbourg, Nova Scotia)

Epaulettes were ordered from 1766, in gold with scarlet silk for artillery companies and in silver with blue silk for the *ouvriers* companies in Haiti and Mauritius.

AUXILIARY COLONIAL TROOPS

Formed in 1756 from deserters from the British Army, the **Irish Corps** were mostly Irish Catholics who sought refuge with the French in Canada and formed a small unit. They were seen at the siege of Fort William Henry in August 1756 wearing red turned up with green. Formed into a company of 50 men from June 1757, they worked on Quebec fortifications until sent to France in September to be incorporated in Irish regiments.

During the short occupation of St John's, Newfoundland, in 1762, a corps of 400-500 Irishmen recruited in the island was organised in August and sent to France.

The **Canadian Volunteers** were a distinct, apparently permanent unit commanded by Captain de Villiers and composed of about 300 Canadian volunteers reported with Montcalm's army in 1757 and 1758. In 1759, it was under Captain de Repentigny. It was a light infantry unit skilled in skirmishing.

In May 1759, a **Corps of Cavalry (Canada)** was organised in Quebec City for permanent service, making it the first regular cavalry to be raised in Canada. It consisted of 200 troopers recruited among Canadians led by five French metropolitan officers. Their commander was Captain de la Roche-Beaucour of the Montcalm Cavalry Regiment, who had come to Canada as General Montcalm's senior aide-de-camp. The corps was a combination of dragoons and light cavalry, and was especially skilled at skirmishing with Anglo-American light troops. It was disbanded at the surrender of Montreal in September 1760. The uniform (Plate D) was blue and red for the men, white for officers.

The **Chasseurs de Gens de Couleur (Haiti)** was a chasseur company recruited from free Blacks and mulattoes. It was ordered raised from 29 April 1762, to serve for the duration of the war. Uniform unknown.

Troops of the 'Compagnie des Indes'

European Troops: When the Compagnie des Indes (French East India Company) was formed in May 1719, it incorporated a number of other commercial companies managing colonies in India, the islands of Mauritius and La Réunion, posts in Senegal and the Guinea Coast in Africa, and Louisiana in America. These various colonies had garrisons which were incorporated into the Company's own military establishment. At first, in 1720, the Company attempted to augment the establishment of garrisons in Louisiana and Mauritius by sending Swiss companies of *Soldats-Ouvriers*. The Swiss were not dependable in such outposts, and their uniforms are unknown.

In order to provide marines for the Company's ships and recruits overseas, a large depot company was created at Lorient in Brittany, on 1 October 1721. At first consisting of 100 men with four officers, it was augmented in 1740 to 300 men and 11 officers. This, however, was just a small part of what was becoming a sizeable establishment.

In **India** in the 1720s, there were four companies in Pondichèry, on the Coromandel coast, and three (two from 1728) in Mahé, on the Malabar coast, each having 80 European officers and men, with 55 *Topas* attached. (Topas were a class of Christian Indian and Portuguese mixed bloods who dressed as Europeans.) The force averaged 375 Europeans and 150 Topas. In the later 1730s, this grew to 800 Europeans and 250 Topas. Companies in Pondichèry were raised to 100 Europeans each in 1738. In the 1740s, the establishment was at about 900 Europeans and 300 Topas, raised to 1200 Europeans in ten companies by 1750. During the early 1750s, many recruits were sent from France, including some 900 Germans raised by J.-C. Fischer, making a total of 3,100 to 3,300 Europeans. There were only 500 Topas, but thousands of Sepoys had been hired by the French.

From the 1720s, the troops were nearly all infantry, with 20 to 30 gunners, but there was more variety from the later 1740s. As General Bussy's army, which operated in central India, showed, grenadiers, volunteers, dragoons, horse grenadiers and artillery companies were raised locally. Among the Germans recruited by Fischer was a company of hussars, and there were a few companies of Portuguese volunteers in Pondichery. Another addition were some Black 'Caffres' brought from Africa. In any event, casualties, sickness, capture and desertion had depleted these troops to 316 including 124 invalids at the surrender of Pondichery on 15 January 1761.

The first regular garrison in **Iles de France et de Bourbon** (Mauritius and La Réunion) was the Swiss company of *Soldats-Ouvriers* which arrived in 1722 and soon proved inept and mutinous. To replace it quickly, royal orders of March and April 1723 raised four companies of 50 men each for the Compagnie des Indes by assigning experienced soldiers from the Piedmont, Richelieu and Artois regiments to form part of the force sent to the islands. In September 1724, one of the two companies at La Réunion was sent to Pondichèry, and a company at Mauritius later

disbanded so that there remained only two companies of 53 men each by 1735. Governor La Bourdonnais raised this to 86 per company in 1737. In 1741, the garrison was sent to Pondichèry, which was then threatened by the Mahratas. During the Seven Years' War, most of the troops appear to have been sent as reinforcements to India. This also included local volunteers embodied into a company of *Volontaires de Bourbon* reportedly uniformed in red. The Company troops left in the islands were joined in 1760 by the Cambrésis Regiment and the last were relieved by the Légion de l'Ile de France from 1767.

Detachments of Company troops from Mauritius and La Réunion were occasionally posted to coastal trade forts on **Madagascar**. In 1756, 100 soldiers were reported there on a punitive expedition against natives.

In **Africa**, Senegal was reinforced in 1723 by six companies of 50 men each posted at Saint-Louis, Goree (near present-day Dakar) and Galam. After a couple of years in a deadly climate, they were much depleted with only 148 officers and men, and down to 86 in 1734. Reinforcements were later sent, as there were 232 officers and soldiers taken by the British at Saint-Louis in May 1758, and about 300 at Goree in December. The post at Ouidha on the Guinea Coast was neutral, like other European slave stations in that area, and had no garrison.

The Company had a factory in Canton in **China** for managing its trade in the Far East. A small guard of the Company's soldiers was posted there from the 1720s to 1771. They were usually detached from ships on a rotating basis.

In 1719, there were 16 companies of 55 officers and men in **Louisiana**; they were reduced to 12 companies each of 50 officers and men in October 1723, down to ten companies in September 1724, and eight companies in December 1725. These troops were detached at Mobile, Biloxi, Fort Toulouse, Dauphine Island, New Orleans, and up the Mississippi River right up to Fort de Chartres in Illinois. The Swiss company in Louisiana from 1720 was much weakened by disease, many deserted, some mutinied and the remnants were disbanded in 1725. In 1731, Louisiana became a royal colony and its troops were incorporated into the colonial Compagnies franches de la Marine.

Uniforms

From the 1720s to the 1760s, the Company's troops had two types of uniform. The first was the 'official' uniform made in France and worn by the depot in Lorient, the marines on board its ships, its garrisons in Senegal and, from 1720 to 1731, in Louisiana. The second type was the uniform clothing made in India and worn by troops there and in the islands in the Indian Ocean (Plates E and G).

The official uniform was similar to that of the Compagnies franches de la Marine except for minor details. It consisted of a grey-white coat with blue cuffs, lining, waistcoat, breeches and stockings, brass buttons, false gold hat lace, white shirt, cravat, gaiters and black shoes. A linen

Kerjean's Volunteers, Bussy's Army, India, 1753. Fur cap with blue bag piped white, blue coat and breeches, red lapels and cuffs, pewter buttons, white aiguillette and gaiters. (Print after L. Rousselot)

15

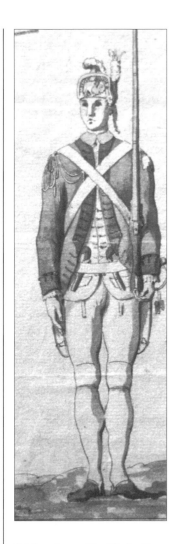

Soldier of an unidentified unit marked 'Troupes servant dans l'Inde. Troupes coloniales 1760' ('Troops serving in India. Colonial troops 1760'). They are dressed in a colourful uniform of red coats with green lapels and cuffs, yellow or buff collars, white lining, waistcoats, breeches, gaiters, aiguillette and epaulettes; the cap seems only partly coloured with yellow trim, and black and white feather. (Archives Nationales)

frock and a pair of linen trousers were also issued to soldiers serving as marines. Clothing bills in the 1740s mention 'white' cloth rather than grey-white, with three dozen large brass buttons per coat, three dozen small buttons per waistcoat, and black instead of white cravats. A blue collar is mentioned as being part of the uniform in 1752. For the garrisons of Senegal, the uniform was the same colour, but made of light materials to counter the great heat. Officers had the same uniform made of better material with more gold buttons and gold hat lace. Those sent to Senegal were advised to have their uniform made of light cloth. This white and blue uniform was worn until 1760.

For troops in India and the Indian Ocean islands, the uniforms were made on the spot from Indian material. These uniforms were very different and far more colourful than the Company's uniforms from France. The early uniforms worn by the troops at Pondichery, Mahé de Malabar and other factories are unknown in any detail except that they were of red cotton or, for the troops at Mahé, of *guingam*, a light cloth, usually dyed blue. In 1727, a coat of red serge with blue cuffs was confirmed for all troops. On 17 May 1737, the board of the Company in Paris ordered the Superior Council of Pondichery to henceforth provide uniforms of 'blue Guingam with red serge cuffs' to the troops. The buttons were brass, the hat lace false gold. Officers had the same but of better quality with gold buttons and hat lace. Red collars were also specified for their uniforms in 1745.

The troops at Mauritius and La Réunion were initially clothed with grey-white and blue uniforms from France but, in 1732, the Company 'forgot' to send uniforms from Lorient so that the men were henceforth clothed with guingam from Pondichery.

In India, the variety of uniforms worn by troops as French power grew under Governor General Dupleix became truly extraordinary. An anonymous soldier with the Marquis de Bussy's army operating in central India between 1751 and 1755 left a blessedly detailed account of the dress of the small French force (Plate G).

Soon after it took the field, he reports in April 1751 that: '...the troops were dressed in the following way: Kerjean's [Dupleix's cousin] Company, blue vest, breeches and [forage] caps, red lapels, cuffs and cap turn-up with a blue fleur-de-lis in front; Grenadier's [Company]: red vest, breeches and [forage] caps, blue lapels, cuffs and cap turn-up with a red fleur-de-lis in front; Volunteers [Company]: blue vest, breeches and [forage] caps, yellow lapels, cuffs and cap turn-up with a blue fleur-de-lis in front; the Artillery, blue coat and breeches, red cuffs, with hats...shirts and white and blue gaiters were also issued...'

Following French successes, their Indian ally Nabob Salabed-Jing made a gift of uniforms to Bussy's men, which were described in June 1751: 'All our troops were dressed with: ...red coats and breeches, green lapels and cuffs, red caps with green turn-ups. On the sergeant's caps [of Kerjean's Company] was a fleur-de-lis with the motto PERICULA LUDUS and a cord around, all embroidered in silver on green, with a silver tassel at the end of the cap. Corporals and fusiliers had the same embroidery in white silk;...the Grenadier's [Company] had only a white cloth grenade; that of the Volunteers had a white rosette, and the artillery had a bomb. As for our Caffres and Topas, they had a red fleurs-de-lis, with a pair of gaiters to each soldier. This clothing gave a very good appearance to our troops.' By October 1751, cavalry had been added, as Bussy wrote to Dupleix about 'our dragoons' wearing very handsome scarlet coats 'with a narrow gold lace' and caps.

Two years later, in June 1753, Bussy's army had grown to 935 Europeans, 55 Topas, 7,800 natives and was as colourful as ever. The General's Guard had: 'red coats laced [with gold], red breeches, green cuffs also laced, gold aiguillettes, bandoleer with red and green squares edged with gold lace and gilt hooks, hat laced with gold and gold buttons'. The dragoons had: 'green coats and breeches, red lapels, cuffs and aiguillettes, green cap with fur and brass buttons'. The artillery had: 'green coats and breeches, red cuffs, red and green caps with a red cannon ball in front, red buttons'. Kerjean's Volunteers had: 'blue coats and breeches, red lapels and cuffs, blue cap with fur and three white laces on the bag, pewter buttons and white aiguillettes'. The company of *Étrangers* (foreigners – deserters led by an English captain) had: 'red coats and breeches, red buttons, yellow lapels and cuffs, red and yellow caps'. The Topas had: 'couleur de chair' (skin colour, usually meaning pink) coat and breeches, red lapels, cuffs and buttons, pink and red caps'. The three French companies had: 'red coat, breeches and red cloth buttons, green lapels and cuffs, red and green caps. These three companies and that of the Foreigners had a red fleur-de-lis in front of the cap. The three French companies forming the *Corps de bataillon* were distinguished by epaulettes. The first had white, the second had green and the third had blue [epaulettes]. All our troops, in battle lines, made a magnificent sight.'

Bussy's men were issued new uniforms in November 1754 except for the *Corps de bataillon* companies. The other companies now had: 'red vests and breeches, green lapels and cuffs, red buttons; the sergeants had red coats, green cuffs edged with a gold lace, no lapels...all were issued hats.' The *Grenadiers à cheval* (horse grenadiers) had: 'blue coats, red lapels and cuffs, brass buttons, all had hats'. Bussy's Guards, 12 strong, wore: 'red coats, green cuffs with a gold lace, gold laced hat, bandoleers with red and green small squares and two gold laces on each side'. The 14 Caffres, some armed with blunderbusses and others with sabres, wore long red robes and red baggy trousers, high hussar caps covered with long-haired bearskin and a silver fleur-de-lis in front.

The guards and Caffres in rich uniforms were a necessary feature of oriental diplomacy with Indian princes who required outlandish displays. The governor-general of French India had a mounted horse guard of 12 Europeans wearing scarlet coats with black cuffs edged gold, their captain having all seams trimmed with gold lace. He also had a militia of native 'Pions' as foot guards for his escort which had to be elaborate at all times. 'When Mr. Dupleix goes out', wrote an observer around 1750, 'he is preceded by six European guards with their captain, all mounted, followed by 12 lance bearers and 24 pions each carrying a gold and white flag, followed by 12 elephants richly decorated, on one of which was a large French standard, on another the sign of Muramat on a large gold and white standard which only the viceroys of the Mogul empire could carry' and two large brass kettle-drums on another, accompanied by trumpeters, fifers 'and other instruments used in India'. Formal parades called for thousands of richly costumed participants on horse and foot with scores of elephants and flags in displays scarcely

Fusilier, French East India Company Infantry, c.1760-1774. Blue coat and breeches, red cuffs, lapels and waistcoat, white buttonhole and hat lace, pewter buttons. This uniform, ordered in 1758, was first worn at Lorient in France from 1760 and at Pondichery and other factories in India from 1765 until 1773. (Print after Marbot)

The *Chevalier Gentil*, a superior officer of the French East India Company's troops, c.1765-1770. He wears the blue uniform ordered for the Company's European troops in 1758 with epaulettes adopted by officers after the Seven Years War. The medal hung on a scarlet ribbon is the cross of Saint-Louis showing that the wearer was a knight of this military order. Blue coat and collar, red lapels, silver buttons, lace and epaulettes. (Print after portrait)

imaginable in Europe. In about 1756, the board of the Compagnie des Indes in France decided that the uniform of the troops in India would be the white and blue 'official' dress. But it was obviously not worn in India. The Superior Council of Pondichery replied on 3 February 1757 that, in effect, it was a nice idea, that the white cloth sent for that purpose would be used when it arrived, but it also advised that, in India, 'a blue uniform is best in these countries because the colour holds better and is less dirty than white'.

This opinion had an effect. On 15 March 1758, the board of the Compagnie des Indes meeting in Paris ruled again on the uniform of its troops. In the future, the uniform of 'all its troops, be they in India, in the islands and at Lorient' would be a blue coat with blue lining and collar, red cuffs and lapels, pewter buttons and white buttonhole lace, red waistcoat with white buttonhole lace, blue breeches and stockings, hat laced with white lace. Sergeants had silver lace edging their cuffs, pocket flaps and hat. Officers had the same uniform but of better quality with silver buttons and lace. This uniform seems to have been taken into wear by the troops at Lorient only in March 1760, and it was certainly never worn in India before it fell to the British in early 1761. It was, however, the dress of the Company's troops in Pondichery and other factories from 1765 until 1773, as well as that of the detachment in Canton, China, and the depot in Lorient until 1774. Officers wore silver epaulettes from about 1763.

There is scant information on the weapons and accoutrements of the Company's soldiers. They were bought in France and shipped to garrisons overseas. A 1751 contract between the Company and the arms factories at St Etienne and Charleville for infantry muskets, rampart muskets and cavalry carbines suggest the same models and calibres as used by the regular army except for brass furnishings. Swords and bayonets were also furnished as in the army. Accoutrements were initially buff with a belly box, but this changed during the 1740s to the 'giberne' style with the cartridge box slung from a buff shoulder belt. An issue in May 1761 mentioned a cartridge box holding 18 to 20 rounds, a sabre and a hatchet to each soldier at Lorient.

Artillery

The Compagnie des Indes had its own small artillery corps. Master gunners were appointed to oversee the artillery and train men in gunnery. Although some forts had many guns (St Louis in Senegal had 94 cannon in the 1750s, for instance), the Company generally depended on some infantrymen trained as gunners and had no distinct artillery units except in India. The exact date of the formation of an artillery company in India is unknown, but, in April 1751, such a unit was described in Bussy's army. A muster of 1753 reveals that the company consisted of 31 European artillerymen, assisted by 159 Indian 'Lascars',

335 wagoners, 18 carpenters and so on. There may have been other artillery companies with General Law's army in the Carnatic and in Pondichery. A small detachment of gunners was noted by the British for putting up a stiff fight at Plassey in 1757. At the surrender of Pondichery in January 1761, the Company's artillery seem to have gathered the remains of two European artillery companies with the infrastructure of a small corps. From 1765 to 1773, a company of artillery was included in the Battalion of India.

The gunners' uniform was generally the same as the Company's European infantry. In April 1751, the European gunners in Bussy's army were described wearing the standard blue coats with red cuffs, blue breeches and tricorn hats. However, there could be some amazing variety in India. By July 1751, they had changed to red coat and breeches, green cuffs and lapels, red cap with green turn-up having a flaming bomb in front. In June 1753, they now had 'green coats and breeches, red cuffs, red and green caps with red cannonballs in front'. A last description in November 1754 mentions Bussy's gunners wearing red vests and breeches, green cuffs and lapels, red cloth buttons and tricorn hats.

The ordnance used by the Company came from various sources. It was allowed to cast its own guns and produced very fine ornate brass cannon. But many more were purchased. In the 1750s for instance, some 360 iron cannon were purchased in Sweden, while another 78 iron cannon and 18 mortars were ordered from Douai, in France.

Sepoys

It was only in 1737 that Sepoys were first hired by the French in Pondichery to provide reinforcement to the small garrison of European soldiers and Topas. From a few hundreds, the corps of Sepoys grew to about 5,000 by the mid-1740s, at which time Dupleix insisted on a more European style of organisation. Companies generally numbered about 100 men including a captain ('soubedar'), an ensign ('alfer'), two sergeants, four corporals and two 'tam-tams' or drummers, and battalions with French officers in senior command posts. As French power increased in southern India, the number of Sepoys in the pay of the Compagnie des Indes rose to about 10,000.

Some Sepoys had elements of uniforms as part of their costume. In the later 1740s, Sepoys of the Pondichery garrison were issued blue jackets with red cuffs. While they liked the idea of uniforms, they did not appreciate the excessive deduction from their pay and did not wish to renew the experiment. In the Nellore area, where some 1,200 Sepoys were posted in the early 1750s, equal quantities of red, blue, yellow and green material were procured to provide uniform jackets for the 12 companies. Three companies had a jacket of one colour with facings at the collar, cuffs and lapels of the other three colours. Thus, three companies would have yellow jackets, one company with red facings, another with green (Plate G) and another with blue; three companies would have red jackets with blue, yellow and green facings, and so on. The cost of the uniform was deducted at a fair price, and the Sepoys liked the idea, especially as it distinguished them

Sepoy, French India, 1740s and 1750s. These troops wore their native costume usually consisting of a white turban, a long-skirted sleeved robe, and long trousers. They had pointed oriental shoes with no heels. They were armed with musket and bayonet, Indian 'talwar' sabre and 'kattary' dagger. In the field, the front of the robe was tucked under the waistbelt. (Print after L. Rousselot)

BELOW **Mulatto chief, Laptots de Goree, Senegal, 1765.** The chiefs acted as officers and wore a European cut uniform: white coat and breeches, yellow collar, cuffs and waistcoat, silver buttons and hat lace, and buff accoutrements. They were armed with musket, bayonet and sword. (Musée de la Marine, Paris)

BOTTOM **Free Black, Laptots de Goree, Senegal, 1765.** The free Blacks acted as sergeants and wore white jackets and breeches, yellow collars, cuffs and waistcoats, silver buttons and hat lace, and buff accoutrements. They were armed with muskets, bayonets and swords. (Musée de la Marine, Paris)

from the more unruly Sepoys of local rajahs. However, no universal uniform was imposed on the Company's Sepoys and they generally wore their native costume.

COLONIAL TROOPS 1763-1772

Following the end of the Seven Years' War, France still had a sizeable number of colonies. The policy of having rotating garrisons of metropolitan army battalions proved immediately impractical in Senegal, Guyana and St Pierre and Miquelon, which were provided with new units of colonial troops from 1763. By 1766, the larger colonies of Haiti, Mauritius and La Réunion were provided with colonial 'Legions' and various auxiliary units. Finally, in 1772-1773, they were replaced by eight colonial infantry regiments.

The **Compagnie franche de Saint-Pierre et Miquelon** was an independent company raised in 1763 to garrison the islands of St Pierre and Miquelon south of Newfoundland, which were used as bases for the French fishing fleet. Uniform similar to the Légion de Saint-Domingue from 1767.

Two companies of **Volontaires d'Afrique** were raised in April 1763 for service in Goree, Senegal. There were three companies from December 1764, reduced to one in March 1767. Uniform from 1767: blue coat, red collar, cuffs, lapels, lining, waistcoat and breeches, pewter buttons, white hat lace.

The **Troupes nationales de Cayenne** were a corps of 20 companies authorised in May 1764, reduced to 12 in October 1765, and to eight in 1771. Uniform from 1764: white coat, blue collar, cuffs, lapels, lining, waistcoat and breeches, brass buttons, gold-laced hat; white lining, waistcoat and breeches from June 1767.

Raised in Goree, Senegal, from 15 September 1765, the **Laptots de Goree** were composed of 82 captive Blacks including 20 Christians, four free Black sergeants, mulatto and white officers. They were disbanded from March 1767. Dressed in white faced yellow and armed in a peculiar fashion (see illustrations).

A first legion of over 500 men, half white and half free Black and mulattos, existed in Haiti from January to September 1765, clothed in white faced with red. On 1 April 1766, a royal order created the **Légion de Saint-Domingue**, 54 companies of 100 men each (including eight gunners and eight grenadiers) of which 14 companies served as a depot at Ile de Ré, France. In April 1769. the legion was reduced to 30 companies of 60 men each, including three companies of gunners and three of grenadiers. Ordered incorporated into the new Du Cap and Port-au-Prince regiments from August 1772. Uniform: blue coat and coat cuffs (three buttons under), red lapels and collar, white turnbacks, waistcoat and breeches, pewter buttons, white hat lace.

Raised from July 1766, the **Légion de l'Ile de France** was to have 30 companies of 100 men each for service in Mauritius and La Réunion with a depot in Lorient. Ordered incorporated into the new colonial infantry regiments in August 1772. Actual incorporation took place in 1773. Uniform: white coat, lining, waistcoat and breeches, blue collar, cuffs and lapels, pewter buttons, white hat lace.

The **Dragons de Saint-Domingue** were three dragoon companies, each with three officers and 100 men, organised from October 1769 for service in Haiti. Disbanded and amalgamated into the new colonial infantry regiments after August 1772, their uniform was the same as the Légion de Saint-Domingue, but with white round hat and boots.

The **Ile de France, Ile de Bourbon, Port-Louis, Du Cap, Port-au-Prince, Martinique** and **Guadeloupe** regiments were raised from August 1772. **Pondichery** and the **Volontaires de Beniowsky** were raised from December 1772. The Ile de Bourbon Regiment was for service at La Réunion, and the Port-Louis Regiment was for service in Mauritius. Neither regiment was recruited to established strength, and both were incorporated into the Ile de France regiment in 1775. Uniform: white coat, lining, waistcoat and breeches, pewter buttons and white hat lace, red collar, cuffs and lapels for Ile de Bourbon, green for Port-Louis. The organisation and dress of the other units is given in MAA 244 *The French Army in the American War of Independence.*

COLONIAL MILITIAS

New France Militias

From the late 1660s in **Canada**, every man able to bear arms from the age of 16 to 60 was enrolled in a company of militia. Each parish had one or more companies, usually numbering about 50 men, and each led by a captain, lieutenants and sergeants. The parish companies belonged to one of the three districts of Quebec, Trois-Rivières and Montreal. Each district had an administrative staff consisting of a colonel, assisted by majors; in wartime, regular colonial officers had overall command. In 1716, the militia amounted to about 4,500 men and this grew to 8,000 by 1734; to some 13,000 including 724 officers divided into 165 companies by 1750; and to over 15,200 ten years later.

A Canadian militia company assembled once a month for muster, and often some target shooting instead of drill. Besides military matters, it was concerned with many local government duties such as the pursuit of criminals and road construction. Generally, only a small proportion of men, usually volunteers, would be detached to serve in military expeditions. They were fierce and outstanding bush fighters and raiders who could move very fast in the wilderness during any season with almost incredible endurance. During the Seven Years' War, however,

TOP **Gourmet, Laptots de Goree, Senegal, 1765. The 20 captive Christian Blacks were called 'Gourmet' and wore a white jacket and breeches, yellow collar, cuffs and waistcoat, pewter buttons, and buff accoutrements. Armed with muskets, bayonets and swords, they also wore a distinctive white cap trimmed with yellow. (Musée de la Marine, Paris)**

ABOVE **Laptot, Laptots de Goree, Senegal, 1765. The 60 captive Muslim Blacks were called 'Laptot' and wore the same uniform as the Gourmets. However, they were only armed with a lance which had a yellow pennon. (Musée de la Marine, Paris)**

This detail from a religious painting showing Canadian militiamen gives a good view of the distinctive costume they wore. The hooded capots are brown and grey and shown with boot cuffs. (Church of Rivière-Ouelle, Quebec)

increasingly large numbers were embodied as the Anglo-American armies approached from all sides. In 1759, nearly all able-bodied men were called out, and some 600 were incorporated into the metropolitan battalions. In 1760, some 2,264 Canadian militiamen were incorporated into the eight metropolitan and two marine battalions, so that 38% of the 'French' regulars were actually Canadians. They all fought with distinction in countless engagements and skirmishes until the surrender of Canada at Montreal in September 1760.

Canadian militiamen had no official military uniform (Plate B). Although they received no pay, clothing and equipment was supplied to the militiamen going on campaign. This generally consisted of a cloth cap which was often red; a 'capot' or hooded coat, usually blue, brown, black, white and sometimes green or wine red; a cloth sash to hold the capot, fastened around the waist of red, grey, black, or green and sometimes adorned with Indian-style beading; breeches or breechclouts; 'mitasses' which were the Indian-style leggings usually in red or white cloth, but also in deerskin; deerskin mitts and moccasins. The armament usually consisted of a light calibre hunting (also used for the fur trade) musket, often made at Tulle, with which many Canadians were outstanding marksmen; a powder horn; a bullet and ammunition pouch; a tomahawk, and often up to three knives: one at the knee garter, one tucked into the sash and another hanging from the neck. Officers were similarly dressed and equipped, but distinguished by a gilt gorget and, when not on campaign in the wilderness, a sword and, frequently in cities, a spontoon.

Gilt officer's gorget of Pierre Trudelle of the Canadian militia. This is the plain, older double bossed gorget used from about the 1720s and apparently the most prevalent type well into the 1760s. Trudelle was killed at the battle of Montmorency, where the British landing was repulsed during the siege of Quebec on 16 July 1759. (Musée des Ursulines, Quebec City)

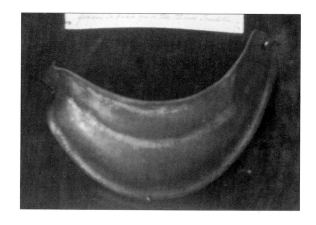

There were a few specialist units. From 1723, about 20 militiamen in Quebec City were trained as gunners, and this unit had grown to a company by 1750. Another militia artillery company had been raised at Montreal by that date. Neither uniform is known. In 1752, Governor-General Duquesne ordered two uniformed bourgeois *Compagnies de Réserve* raised, one in Quebec City and one in Montreal (Plate D). A company of militia *Ouvriers* was raised in 1759 to serve as firemen in Quebec City. Finally, some of the men enlisted in the regular battalions in 1759 and 1760 were apparently issued French regimental uniforms.

The militia was far less important in **Ile Royale**. Only in 1740 were two companies organised at Louisbourg, four more, and perhaps as many as seven, being organised during the 1745 siege. Port Toulouse also had a company. There is little evidence of a sustained organisation between 1749 and 1758, although numerous townsmen assisted the regulars in the second siege of Louisbourg.

The panic caused by the capture of Fort Rosalie by Natchez Indians in 1729 provoked the first serious organisation of militias in **Louisiana**.

LEFT **Gentleman-cadet, Gardes de la Marine, c.1720. The young aspiring naval officers were armed with shorter muskets for drills and were schooled in various naval and military topics. (Private collection)**

RIGHT **Captain, Gardes du Pavillon Amiral, *c.*1717 wearing an all-scarlet uniform with gold buttons and lace. The cadets had lace at the cuffs and pocket flaps, and lace also edged the coats of the officers. (Bibliothèque Nationale)**

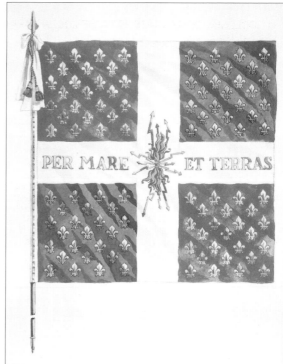

Gentleman-cadet, Gardes du Pavillon Amiral, c.1732, wearing a blue coat, red cuffs, lining, waistcoat, breeches and stockings, gold buttons and lace edging the cuffs and pocket flaps, buff belts, reddish brown cartridge box. (Bibliothèque Nationale)

Four companies were organised in New Orleans and others were formed from free Black companies in New Orleans in 1739, and in Mobile from the 1740s. An artillery company was organised in Mobile in 1746. In the plantation settlement of lower Louisiana, the West Indies militia organisation was adopted. In upper Louisiana (or Illinois), which had been settled by Canadians, the Canadian-style parish militia was favoured. In the 1730s and 1740s, substantial numbers of Louisiana militiamen assisted the regulars in expeditions against hostile Indians. They generally had no uniforms, although Governor Vaudreuil mentioned in 1751 that many in lower Louisiana wished to have uniforms like in the West Indies.

West Indies and Guyana Militias

The militia of the French West India islands and Guyana was to include all white men able to bear arms, but a few companies of free Blacks were also raised as time went on. They usually had white officers, but Black officers led the company of free Blacks at Le Cap in Haiti. Generally, all white infantry militiamen were each to have a musket with bayonet, a cartridge box and a sabre or sword; cavalrymen or dragoons a musket with bayonet, a pair of pistols, and a broadsword. In addition, each white militiaman could be accompanied by a trusted Black slave armed with a buccaneer musket. As with all militias in colonies with large slave populations, the prevention of slave uprisings and internal security was often more important than defence against external enemies.

COLONIAL COMPAGNIES FRANCHES DE LA MARINE 1749-60
1: Officer
2: Sergeant
3: Cadet à l'aiguillette
4: Drummer
5: Private

CANADIAN MILITIA & AUXILIARIES c.1715-60
1: Indian Warrior
2: Officer
3: Militiaman, cold weather campaign
4: Militiamen in summer campaign

CANONNIERS-BOMBARDIERS 1750-60
1: Officers
2: Gunner
3: Gun crew
4: Sergeant

CORPS IN CANADA 1750s-60
1: Trooper, Corps of Cavalry, 1759-1760
2: Fusilier, Compagnies franches de la Marine, outposts
3: Sergeant, Compagnies franches de la Marine Battalion, 1757-1760
4: Militiaman, 'Royal-Syntaxe' Company, 1759
5: Militiaman, Milice de Réserve, 1752-1760

AFRICA AND THE INDIAN OCEAN
1: Fusilier, French East India Company Troops, 1720s-1737
2: Fusilier, French East India Company Troops, c.1750
3: Habitant, Ile de France and Ile de Bourbon Militia, 1740s-1750s
4: Dragoon, Ile de France and Ile de Bourbon Militia, 1740s-1750s
5: Gendarme, Ile de France and Ile de Bourbon Militia, 1740s-1750s

E

WEST INDIES
1: Private, de la Roche's Battalion, Martinique, 1761-1762
2: Officer with colour, Company of Fusiliers, Du Cap Militia, Haiti, 1740
3: Fusilier, Karrer's (Swiss) Regiment (Hallwyl's from 1752) c.1740-63
4: Trooper, Gendarmes of Saint-Pierre, Martinique c.1740-1762
5: Trooper, Captain Demassin's Company of Dragoons, Martinique, 1761-1762

F

INDIA
1: Fusilier, 1st French Company, Bussy's Army, 1751-1755
2: Fusilier, European Infantry, French East India Company,
c.1737-1750
3: Fusilier, Company of Topas, Bussy's Army, 1753-1754
4: Sepoy, Nellore District, c.1750-1755
5: Trooper, Company of Bussy's Guards, 1753-1755

G

NAVAL TROOPS
1: Fusiliers, Compagnies franches des Galères (galley marines), c.1740
2: Garde de l'Étendart réal des Galères c.1740
3: Capitaine d'armes, Compagnies franches
de la Marine (ship marines), c.1740
4: Gunner, Bombardier de la Marine, c.1754

LEFT *Ordonnance* colour of the Compagnies franches de la Marine after a description of 1737. The first and fourth quarters are red, the second and third are blue, white cross with *PER MARE ET TERRAS* (by sea and by land), thunderbolts and flames in natural colours, lilies and letters in gold. The Colonel's colour (the British equivalent would be the King's colour) had all quarters and the cross in white with the same devices as on the *Ordonnance* (or 'regimental') colour. Reconstitution by Michel Pétard. (Canadian Dept. of National Defence)

In 1705, the militia companies of the French West Indies and Guyana were grouped into seven regiments in Haiti, four in Martinique, two in Guadeloupe, one in Grenada and two at Cayenne in Guyana. The regiments were mainly composed of infantry, but might also include cavalry. From 1727 to 1732, the regimental organisation was abolished and the companies were attached to their local districts and parishes. Ideally, these local area militia organisations had companies of white infantry and cavalry or dragoons, with others made up of free Blacks and mulattoes.

The early militiamen of **Saint-Domingue (Haiti)** were often buccaneers and rough-and-tumble planters. In 1705, the companies were grouped into seven infantry regiments and, in 1710, a cavalry regiment was raised in the northern district. The regiments were abolished in 1732 and the militia organisation reverted to independent companies of infantry, cavalry and dragoons. Militia artillery seems to have been formed at Le Cap, but elsewhere, such companies seem to date only from 30 October 1755 when the governor-general ordered a company formed in the towns of Port-au-Prince, Petit-Gouave, Saint-Louis and Saint-Marc. Following the Seven Years' War, the militia was disbanded in 1764, raised for a few months in 1765, and re-raised by royal order from 1 April 1768.

From the beginning of the 18th century militia cavalry officers wore, 'blue and red uniforms' which appears to have meant a blue coat with red cuffs and lining. Militia infantry officers wore, from about 1710, white coats, with red collars, cuffs and lining. The ordinary militiamen had no uniforms initially. However, as the cities of the colony became larger and more prosperous, uniformed units appeared.

Le Cap (now Cap-Haitien) was then the largest and richest city in Haiti. Its first uniformed companies appeared in the 1730s. Thanks to the chronicler, Moreau de Saint-Méry, the uniforms of the companies are known. The first unit in uniform at Le Cap was the company of grenadiers formed in 1732. It had white coats, waistcoats and breeches,

Marine drummer and officer of the Compagnies franches de la Marine based at Le Havre, 1718. The drummer wears the king's livery. The officer wears a grey-white coat with blue cuffs, lining, waistcoat, breeches and stockings, gold lace edging the front of the coat, the cuffs, pocket flaps, waistcoat and hat, gold buttons and gorgets. The notations refer to rank distinctions approved on 19 December 1718. Captains and lieutenants were to have the uniform shown, the *Capitaines d'armes* to have the same as sergeants, sergeants were to wear laces on the cuffs only without edging, soldiers to have only buttons with buff waistbelt and cartridge box of Russia leather. (Montreal Public Library)

scarlet cuffs, collars and lapels, and silver buttons. A company of carabiniers was formed a few years later and wore scarlet coats laced with
silver, with blue cuffs, collars, lapels and lining, and silver buttons. The
company of fusiliers, formed in 1740, wore blue, red and gold, and
carried a colour (Plate F). The company of dragoons raised in the same
period had a blue uniform laced gold, with red cuffs and collars, white
waistcoats and breeches, gold laced hats, gold aiguillettes, and blue
housings laced gold.

From 1768 and during the 1770s, many new units and uniforms
appeared. The mounted gendarmes had scarlet coats, black velvet
collars, cuffs and lapels, gold buttons and lace, and scarlet housings
laced gold. The grenadiers, the carabiniers and the four companies of
fusiliers wore blue coats with white collars, cuffs, linings, waistcoats and
breeches, and silver buttons. The artillery company had blue coats, red
collars, cuffs and lining, white waistcoats and breeches, and gold buttons.
The company of volunteers had scarlet coats, green velvet collars,
cuffs and lapels, green linings, white waistcoats and breeches, gold lace
on coats, and gold buttons. The company of foot dragoons wore
green coats and lining, red collars and cuffs, white waistcoats and
breeches, gold buttons, black cockade and plume, and black gaiters. The
company of chasseurs wore buff coats and lining, Saxon green collars
and cuffs, white waistcoats and breeches, silver buttons, and black
leather gaiters. The company of mulattoes 'and other mixed bloods' had
blue coats, yellow collars, cuffs, lapels and lining,
white waistcoat and breeches, silver buttons. The
company of free Blacks had blue coats, scarlet
collars and cuffs, white linings, waistcoats and
breeches, and silver buttons. The dragoons kept
the same uniform colours as before. There was
also a small militia staff consisting of a com-
mandant, a major and an aide-major, who wore
blue coats with white collars, cuffs, waistcoats and
breeches, gold lace and buttons.

Not all militiamen enjoyed such luxuries as
those of Le Cap. The less affluent southern town
of Léogane reportedly had 'a few braves' in 1748
which had grown to a company of cavalry, one of
artillery, one of carabiniers, four of white infantry,
one of free mulattoes and two of free Blacks by
1762. Perhaps some had uniforms, but they were
reported often badly armed when they had
weapons at all.

Martinique had a militia from the middle of
the 17th century. In 1738, it had some 5,000 men
including 300 free Blacks and mulattoes. In 1761,
there were over 5,000 men and 3,000 armed black
slaves mobilised. Adjoining the land militia were
some 'flibustiers' (freebooters) who formed a sort
of volunteer naval militia, some 4,000 being
mobilised in late 1761. The parish organisation
prevailed, but by 1715, there were special companies of grenadiers and mounted gendarmes.

The Martinique militia was occasionally involved in expeditions on nearby islands, such as punitive raids against Caribs in St Vincent. The French took formal possession of **St Lucia** in 1719, and many Martinique militiamen were detached and settled there from the early 1720s. From 1756, 300 Martinique militiamen were posted in St Lucia and 200 rein-forced **Guadeloupe** in 1759. In October 1761, shortly before the British attack, the Martinique militia was put on a war footing and eight infantry battalions, including one of freebooters, one of free Blacks and some dragoon companies, were organised.

Generally, Martinique militiamen do not seem to have worn uniforms until the middle of the 18th century. The first may have been the Gendarmes of St Pierre, a smart mounted bourgeois company raised in 1716 and uniformed in light grey-blue, red and gold (Plate F). In 1741 most officers at the parish of La Trinité in Martinique were reported in uniform. The governors of other islands were instructed to encourage their militia officers to do the same. The style of these uniforms remains unknown. In October 1761, the Martinique militia battalions were uni-formed, all probably in blue with various facings (Plate F). The battalions also had colours which were blessed on 12 November 1761. De Cour's dragoon company was dressed in a 'green uniform, white cuffs and lapels', and Demassin's dragoon company was in blue, pink and silver. Following the end of the war and the return of the islands to France, the militiamen of Martinique and St Lucia were to wear, from 13 May 1765, blue waistcoats and breeches, cuffs of the colour chosen by the quarters, and gold buttons. Officers also had a blue coat. The dragoons had the same as officers, with blue housings laced yellow, and dragoon officers also had a silver lace. The Gendarmes adopted a red uniform with black

collars, cuffs and lapels edged with gold lace, gold buttons with gold buttonhole lace, and gold laced hats with white plumes.

Guadeloupe had about 2,500 militiamen in the middle of the 18th century, Marie-Galante about 250 and Grenada about 400. The Guadeloupe militia put up a resolute fight in 1759 until the island fell. Grenada surrendered in 1762 and was ceded to Britain in 1763. Almost nothing is known of the dress of the militias until after the Seven Years' War. In 1765, most militia infantry units on the islands of Guadeloupe and Marie-Galante, its smaller neighbour, were assigned a white uniform so that they would resemble regulars. The infantry of Basse-Terre had white coats, waistcoats and breeches, with black cuffs, lapels and collar, and brass buttons, for example; the infantry at Cul-de-Sac had white cuffs with yellow collars and lapels; the infantry on Marie-Galante had crimson collar, cuffs and lapels, etc. All localities had dragoon companies in green coats, waistcoats and breeches, and brass buttons. The company at Les Abimes had buff collars, cuffs and lapels, and the facings of the dragoons at Basse-Terre were black, those at Marie-Galante crimson, and those at Port-Louis red. There were free Black companies at Le Mancenillier on Guadeloupe and at Marie-Galante, both having blue coats, waistcoats and breeches, with blue collars, cuffs and lapels, and brass buttons. The only artillery company in Guadeloupe was at Le Mancenillier, and they wore blue coat and breeches, with red collars, cuffs, lapels and waistcoats, and brass buttons. The artillery at Marie-Galante had an all-blue uniform with brass buttons.

In **French Guyana** in the early 18th century, the militia consisted of only two companies in Cayenne. It grew to three companies by 1762, totalling 125 men, and was disbanded in 1763-1764. Although the schemes to send thousands of settlers to French Guyana in the mid-1760s largely failed, the colony did increase to five districts including Cayenne. On 30 December 1769, a royal order re-established the militia in companies of infantry, dragoons, and artillery for white men, and chasseurs for mulattoes and free Blacks. Each district had at least a company of infantry and one of chasseurs. The dragoons and two artillery companies were in Cayenne.

The December 1769 order specified uniforms. Infantry officers were to have a grey-white linen coat, waistcoat and breeches, sky blue collars, cuffs (three buttons) and lapels (five buttons, four below), silver buttons and a hat laced silver. Dragoon officers were to have a blue linen coat, waistcoat and breeches, buff cuffs, collar and lapels, silver buttons and hat lace. All ranks of the artillery were to have a blue linen coat, waistcoat and breeches, black cuffs, collar and lapels, brass buttons and yellow hat lace. The Chasseurs were to have a green ample vest and breeches, black cuffs, collar and lapels, pewter buttons and white hat lace.

East Indies and Africa
Iles de France et de Bourbon: The militia at La Réunion was the only military force in the colony until 1722 when regular troops were posted there. Mauritius was settled by the French from 1715,

but it seems that the two first companies of militia were only organised in the later 1730s by the energetic governor, Mahé de La Bourdonnais. Most of the early militiamen of La Réunion wore their own peculiar and comfortable clothing: a linen shirt and pantaloons or breeches, a waistcoat and sometimes a coat of light material, a bandanna tied at the back of the head, and a hat. They often went without shoes or stockings due to the heat. Many lived and hunted in the hills and were renowned as superb marksmen.

The growth of the islands' population and their militias was rapid, and in August 1742, the militia was divided into four classes corresponding roughly to the islands' social and economic order. The first class was the Gendarmes, gathering the 'most notable' inhabitants, each of which could be accompanied by four trusty Blacks armed with lances and equipped with axes, picks and shovels to dig entrenchments. The second were the dragoons accompanied by two Blacks. The third was the infantry of which each white man was to be accompanied by an armed Black. The fourth class was 'formed from the poor [white] inhabitants, overseers and servants, with a few chosen Blacks' to serve the artillery. It appears that each island had a company of gendarmes, one of dragoons and several of infantry. The 1742 order contained amazingly detailed instructions regarding the uniforms, equipment and weapons of the militia (Plate E).

Gendarmes had a scarlet coat and breeches, black velvet cuffs, '28 brandebourgs' of gold, gold buttons, a hat laced with gold set in saw-tooth and white plume edging, buckled leather gaiters, a buff sword belt edged with gold lace, a powder horn with a red silk cord, a morocco leather cartridge box edged with gold lace, a saddle covered with crimson velvet seat, scarlet housings edged with a wide and a narrow gold lace, a silver-hilted sword and a cavalry pistol.

Dragoons had a green coat and breeches, scarlet cuffs, gold buttons, hats laced with gold, laced leather gaiters, buff sword belts, morocco leather cartridge boxes, powder horns with a green cord, saddles covered with green seats, green housings edged with a wide gold lace, silver-hilted swords, cavalry carbines and pistols.

The infantry *habitants* had a coat and breeches of blue 'guigam' Indian cloth with small checks, scarlet cuffs, silver buttons, hats laced silver, buff sword belts, morocco leather cartridge boxes, powder horns with a blue cord, silver-hilted swords, and muskets with a sling.

Neither the fourth class, nor the Blacks that accompanied the white militiamen of all classes wore uniforms.

This organisation remained basically in place until the end of the Seven Years' War when the militia was disbanded. On 1 August 1768, an ordinance re-established the militias with a dragoon company on each island, squads of gunners to serve the coastal batteries and a white and a free Black infantry company in each district.

The posts and 'factories' in mainland India and Africa had no permanent militias. Employees of the French East India Company were organised in a militia of sorts during the British siege of Pondichery in 1747. Used to a 'softer' lifestyle, the employees served 'with an indecency that cannot be expressed' reported Dupleix. And their service was not too inspired during the 1760-1761 siege. In Senegal, the British also encountered a hastily raised militia of Company employees and free Blacks in 1758.

NAVAL TROOPS

The **Gardes de la Marine** were naval academies which trained midshipmen who would eventually be commissioned as officers in the French Navy. There were three companies, one each posted in the three naval bases of Brest, Rochefort and Toulon of 60 or more cadets. They received part of their training in the ports and were detached to serve on board warships. They wore blue coats with red cuffs, lining, waistcoats, breeches and stockings, gold buttons, gold laced hats, and buff belts edged with gold lace. From 1740 hats had white plume borders and white cockades. NCOs had gold lace on the cuffs. Drummers wore the king's livery with the grand livery lace.

The **Gardes du Pavillon Amiral** was formed in November 1716, and was an honorific senior cadet company. Eighty, later 60, selected youths from the three Gardes de la Marine companies were chosen to act as guards of the Admiral of France. Initially, its uniform was scarlet coats, linings, waistcoats, breeches and stockings, with blue cuffs, gold buttons, gold lace edging the cuffs and pocket flaps, and gold laced hats. From July 1732, the uniform was blue with scarlet, similar to the Gardes de la Marine, except for added gold lace edging the cuffs and pocket flaps. Hats had a white plume border and white cockade from 1740. Drummers wore the king's livery with the grand livery lace.

The **Compagnies franches de la Marine (Marines)** were raised from 1690; in 1715 there were 100 companies of 35 men each, raised to 45 men in October 1719, reduced to 30 men in December 1725. Reduced to 50 companies of 60 men each in January 1727, numbers were raised to 80 men in December 1733, reduced to 60 men in May 1736, back up to 80 men in December 1739, raised to 60 companies in September 1740, raised to 100 companies of 50 men each in December 1748, raised to 100 men per company in July 1755, reduced to 50 men in December 1759, and finally disbanded on 5 November 1761.

The officers, a captain and a lieutenant per company, held naval commissions so that a captain of a Compagnie franche was also an ensign in the Navy. The companies were divided into three divisions corresponding to France's

Officers of the Marine artillery corps at right wearing red coats with blue cuffs, collar, lining, waistcoat and breeches, silver buttons and hat lace, showing the artillery park to a portly official in civilian dress, c.1755. Naval officers in blue coats with red facings stand behind the official and officers. (Print after details by Vernet)

main naval bases of Rochefort, Brest and Toulon. Each division could be subdivided into smaller ports: Brest had companies posted in Le Havre, for example. Each company furnished detachments that served on board warships. The marines were thus everywhere and participated in every naval engagement until 1761. They could also be formed into temporary battalions as in 1740 for the expedition against the Chickasaw Indians of Louisiana, or the defence of Provence in 1746. Marines on ships in far-flung colonies, such as Louisbourg in 1758, were grouped into small battalions. They were generally considered good, reliable troops.

The uniform of the sea-soldiers was, from 1716, identical to that of the colonial Compagnies franches de la Marine described above. There were very soon, however, some slight differences. As early as 1718, an illustration of a soldier from a company posted in Rochefort shows a small grey-white standing collar with a small brass button on the coat. The 1740 register mentioned the small standing grey-white collar and also grey-white cuffs (Plate H). These distinctions appear to have been for the companies based in Rochefort until about 1750.[2] Elsewhere, the uniform appears to have had blue cuffs and no collar until the mid-1740s. In January 1744, blue turn-down collars are requested for the coats of the companies based in Brest, a practice that seems to have been followed by all shipboard Compagnies franches. Another addition to the coat, seen as early as 1754 on a painting showing a marine in Marseille, was a small white cloth anchor at the point of each turnback. Forage caps could vary wildly, but appear to have been usually grey-white with a blue turn-up, although all blue was also possible, with fleurs-de-lis or an anchor being the most likely badge in front. Gaiters, white or grey, came into wear in the 1740s.

The armament and equipment was the same as the colonial companies except that, from the late 1740s, the *giberne* replaced the belly box.

In late 1760, the uniform of the Compagnie franches for warships (not those in the colonies) was changed to a blue coat with red collar, cuffs, lining, waistcoat and breeches, brass buttons and false gold hat lace. This was to be their last uniform until disbandment in November 1761.

From 1718, the rank badges of sergeants and the *capitaine d'armes* were identical: gold laces on the cuff's buttonholes only. But the *capitaine d'armes* was a senior NCO holding a peculiar function on board warships as he was responsible for weapons and ammunition so, in 1727, additional gold lace edging the top of their cuffs was approved. Drummers wore the king's livery of blue lined red with the small livery lace. Officers

French naval artillery iron 24 pdr. cannon mounted on a wooden naval carriage. The same type of carriage was also used in coastal and colonial forts minus the blocks and tackles which were necessary aboard ships. (Battle of the Restigouche National Historic Site, Restigouche, Quebec)

French naval artillery cannon balls were sometimes stamped with a fleur-de-lis. This example is from the frigate *Le Machault* sunk in 1760. (Battle of the Restigouche National Historic Site, Restigouche, Quebec)

2 The clothing in store at Rochefort in 1751 has blue cuffs as does subsequent records and illustrations. The 1758 register (*État militaire de France*) still mentions the grey-white cuffs and small standing collar but the otherwise reliable compiler merely copied, word for word, Lemau de la Jaisse's 1740 *Abrégé*, probably because he lacked the information. The later registers have reliable descriptions.

had the same uniform as the men, but of better quality with more buttons and, occasionally, gold lace on the waistcoat.

The **Corps de l'Artillerie de la Marine**, or Marine Artillery, was a separate corps, completely independent from the Army's Royal-Artillerie (see MAA 304 *Louis XV's Army Vol. 3*). Its protocolary Grand Master was the Admiral of France and was headed by three *Commissaires généraux* (General Commissioners) with about 40 officers who supervised the companies of bombardiers and of *apprentis canonniers* (apprentice gunners) in each of the three large naval bases of Brest, Rochefort and Toulon.

These officers also designed and supervised the casting of guns for the Navy which were different to those of the Army. Naval guns were nearly all made of iron by Louis XV's reign. The calibres were 4, 6, 8, 12, 18, 24 and 36-pounders. These guns were used in warships, in coastal fortifications in France and in French colonies in America.

From 1759, the responsibility for coastal fortification was transferred to the Army and, on 5 November 1761, the Marine Artillery was amalgamated into Royal-Artillerie. However, the distinct needs of naval artillery were recognised again from 1766 when new companies of apprentice gunners were formed and, from January 1767, the Navy recovered the management of its artillery.

The **Bombardiers de la Marine** (Bombardiers of the Navy) were raised from 1682, in three companies, one for each major naval base of Brest, Rochefort and Toulon. Strength varied from 25 enlisted men in peace, to 50 in war in each company led by a captain, a lieutenant and a sub-lieutenant. This was the French Navy's élite corps of marine artillery. They originally specialised in serving bomb ketches, but their role evolved as instructors for training ship's gunners; a few would also be found in major warships. Some would occasionally be sent to the colonies for particular training duties such as the dozen men sent to Louisbourg in early 1758 to help form the second company of colonial *canonniers-bombardiers*. On 5 November 1761, the three bombardier companies were amalgamated into the Royal-Artillerie.

When Louis XV became king, the uniform was a red coat and breeches, blue cuffs, lining, waistcoat and stockings, silver buttons (four dozen per coat and three dozen small per waistcoat), and silver hat lace

Private, Bombardiers de la Marine, *c.*1718. Red coat and breeches, blue cuffs, lining, waistcoat and stockings, silver buttons, silver lace edging hat, buff waistbelt, reddish brown cartridge box flap with silver grenade, buff powder horn sling, black cravat and cockade. (Anne S.K. Brown Military Collection, Brown University. Photo: R. Chartrand)

with a black cockade. For full dress they had an elaborate blue cap edged with white lace with a sheepskin turn-up ornamented by an embroidered tiger's head in front. In the later 1730s the colour of the breeches was changed to blue. The order of February 1750 added a blue collar to the coat. The cap now looked similar to a bearskin fur grenadier cap with the tiger's head at bottom, a silver flaming bomb badge above and a blue bag with a red tassel (Plate H).

In late 1760, the uniform was changed to a blue coat with red collar, cuffs, lining, waistcoat, breeches and stockings, brass buttons set in pairs on coat and waistcoat from neck to below the waist (six to each coat pocket, four to each cuff), orange buttonholes on the left side of waistcoat only, gold laced hat, blue and orange sabre knot. The fur cap was the same except for a brass bomb badge and orange lace trim and tassel on the bag.

Sergeants were initially distinguished by two silver laces at each cuff and pocket, the corporals with one lace. By the late 1730s, this had changed to a wide silver lace edging the coat cuffs and pockets as well as their waistcoat; corporals had a narrow silver lace edging the coat cuffs and pockets only, and narrow silver cord at the waistcoat's buttonholes. The lace and tassels on the sergeants' cap badge were silver. From 1760, there was double gold lace on the sergeants' coat cuffs, waistcoats and a gold-plated cap badge, with gold lace and tassel on the cap; corporals had single gold lace. Drummers wore the blue and lined red royal livery trimmed with the king's grand livery lace. Officers wore the same as the men, but made of better material.

The **Régiment Étranger de Dunkerke**, or 'Foreign Regiment of Dunkirk', was a short-lived marine unit of 'soldier-sailors' raised from 1 February 1762. Disbanded on 19 March 1763, it had 16 companies of 100 men each recruited from among foreign sailors. The officers could be French or foreign with naval experience. The officers' uniform was blue with red collar, cuffs and lapels 'in the sailor style', and lined white, with a red waistcoat and breeches, blue stockings, the collar and cuffs edged by a narrow silver lace, the lapels having each seven silver buttonhole laces, two below and three to each pocket flap, silver buttonholes and lace edging the waistcoat, silver epaulettes, hat laced silver, white sash. Petty officers had the same dress, but generally without lace. The soldier-sailors had a short blue coat with red collar, cuffs and lapels, white bone buttons, a pair of blue and a pair of white breeches, blue stockings, red sash and a round hat. Drummers had a cassock of the king's livery.

Post-1763 Marine Units

Following the Seven Years' War, a number of Army regiments were assigned to provide detachments of soldiers to serve as marines, an arrangement which proved unsatisfactory. In 1766, two brigades of Royal-Artillerie who had formerly been naval artillerymen, were assigned exclusively marine duties. Augmented and reorganised into three brigades in October 1769, each brigade had a company of bombardiers, four of gunners and three of fusiliers. An increasing number of marines were needed, and eight regiments were created in February 1772 incorporating the previous brigades. These regiments were disbanded in December 1774 and replaced by 100 companies of the new *Corps Royal d'Infanterie de la Marine* and three companies of bombardiers.

The uniform of Royal-Artillerie was worn from November 1761 until 1772 when the distinct marine regimental uniforms were adopted (see illustration).

Galley Fleet Troops

The **Gardes de l'Étendard Royal des Galères** (Guards of the Galley's Royal Standard) had 30 cadets aspiring to be galley officers and also acted as the general's guards in Marseille. It traditionally had an all-scarlet uniform laced with gold. From July 1728, the uniform was a scarlet coat, lining, waistcoat and breeches, black velvet cuffs, gold buttons, white stockings, hat laced gold with a white plume edging and white cockade. By 1740, the cuffs and lining had changed to blue and the stockings to scarlet (Plate H). Drummers wore the king's livery with the grand livery lace. The unit was disbanded in 1748.

The troops of the **Compagnies franches des Galères** provided detachments of marines for the galley fleet in the Mediterranean. Generally, there was one company per galley. From 1715, there were only 15 galleys kept in service at Marseille. Each company had a captain, a lieutenant and an ensign with, 100 NCOs and fusiliers including a drummer. From February 1716, each company was to have 10 grenadiers, a proportion of one in ten that may have been reduced according to the number of men in the companies. In May 1736, the strength of the 15 companies was reduced to 50 men each. From 1744, some 525 men were transferred from Marseille to Toulon to reinforce its garrison as well as to serve as marines on board sailing warships. The establishment of each company was raised by 15 men in November 1746. On 27 September 1748, the galley fleet was officially abolished, and its soldiers incorporated into the ship marines. From about 1716, the uniform was a grey-white coat, with red cuffs, lining, waistcoat, breeches and stockings, brass buttons, a hat laced with a false gold border and a white cockade (Plate H). Drummers wore the king's livery with the small livery lace.

Besides the marines, each galley was to have eight **Pertuisanniers des Galères**, or 'partisan bearers' led by a sergeant whose duty it was to keep a close watch on the convicts. They wore a blue coat with red cuffs, lining, breeches and stockings, pewter buttons, hats laced silver and were armed with a sabre and a partisan.

SELECT BIBLIOGRAPHY

Manuscripts: Archives Nationales (France), Colonies, series A (orders), B (instructions and outgoing correspondence), C2 (East Indies), C8A (Martinique), C9A (Saint-Domingue), C11A (Canada), C11B (Ile Royale), C13A (Louisiana), D2C (Colonial Troops), F1A (Finances), F3 (Moreau de St Méry legislative coll.); Archives Nationales, Marine, series A1 (orders), B2 (instructions and outgoing correspondence), G5 (artillery); Rochefort Naval Archives, series 1E (instructions and correspondence) and 5E2 (Contracts); Lorient Naval

Private, Bombardiers de la Marine, Rochefort, 1734. Red coat and breeches, blue cuffs, lining, waistcoat and stockings, silver buttons, buff waistbelt, reddish brown cartridge box flap with gold grenade and red flames, buff powder horn sling, white cravat. Blue cap edged white with white tassel, black fur turban, silver grenade with red flame on red background edged white with an embroidered tiger's head in front. (Private collection)

Archives, Compagnie des Indes records; Departmental Archives of La Réunion, series Co; National Archives of Canada, journals and papers of officers Bourlamarque, Levis, Montcalm, de la Pause, etc.; Archives nationales du Québec, series NF 25, Montreal probate records; The Henry E. Huntington Library, Vaudreuil Papers.

Publications:

Back, Francis, 'Le capot canadien: ses origines et son évolution au XVIIe et XVIIIe siècles' *Canadian Folklore Canadien*, X, 1988, Nos. 1-2.

Boudriot, Jean, *Compagnie des Indes 1720-1770*, Paris, 1983.

Chartrand, René, *Canadian Military Heritage: Vol. 1, 1000-1754*, Montreal, 1993.

Coste, Gabriel, *Les anciennes troupes de la Marine*, Paris, 1893.

Denoix, L., and Muraciolle, J.-N., *Historique de l'Artillerie de la Marine de ses origines à nos jours*, Paris, 1964.

Dépréaux, Albert, *Les uniformes des troupes de la Marine, coloniales et nord-africaines*, Paris, 1931.

Dessalles, Adrien, *Histoire générale des Antilles*, Vol. 5, Paris, 1848.

Nicolai, Martin L., 'A Different Kind of Courage: The French Military and the Canadian Irregular Soldier during the Seven Years' War', *Canadian Historical Review*, LXX, 1989, No. 1.

Mason, Paul, *Les galères de France, 1481-1781*, Paris, 1936.

Moreau de Saint-Méry, M.-L.-É., *Loix et constitutions des colonies françaises de l'Amérique sous le vent*, Paris, 1784-1790, 6 Vols.

Petitjean-Roger, Jacques, 'Les troupes du roi à la Martinique 1664-1762' *Revue historique de l'Armée*, 1963

Rufz, E., *Études historiques et statistiques sur la population de la Martinique*, Saint-Pierre, Martinique, 1850 (2 Vols.)

Steele, Ian K., *Guerrillas and Grenadiers: The Struggle for Canada, 1689-1760*, Toronto, 1969.

Marine private, Bordeaux Marine Regiment, 1772-1774. The eight marine regiments raised in 1772 had a blue coat with white turnbacks, waistcoat and breeches, pewter buttons and white hat lace. The collar, cuffs and lapels were, for the Brest Regiment: scarlet; Toulon Regiment: yellow; Rochefort Regiment: green; Marseille Regiment: white; Bayonne Regiment: black; Saint-Malo: sky blue; Le Havre Regiment: buff. The Bordeaux Regiment's crimson facings were of a wine-red hue, most suitable for a unit from the celebrated wine area. (Print after Lattré)

ADDENDA TO THE PREVIOUS VOLUMES IN THIS SERIES

Volume 1 The illustration of the Musketeers of the Guard in 1760 shows a detail of the soubreveste covering the upper coat sleeves, a detail not shown in other depictions. It may only have been featured in the issue of the soubreveste given at that time or else is the artist's interpretation of the garment.

Volume 2 Plate A on the Gardes-Françaises shows figures with blue breeches rather than the red mentioned in the army registers. However, blue is shown in the figures of the 1757 manuscript, the source for most of the figures on this plate. Plate E, figure 3. The sergeant of the Ponthieu Regiment could also have cuff lace of mixed silver and gold or plain silver besides the gold shown. The regulations did not specify this distinction in the case of regiments with both silver and gold buttons and lace. Plate F, figure 3. The buttons and lace on the uniform of the officer of Guyenne should be gold.

Volume 3 Pages 16-17. It has been documented, since the book appeared, that the grenadiers of Royal-Écossais wore British-style tallo and pointed grenadier caps in 1745. For details and colour reproduction of an officer's cap, see Stephen Wood's article in the Journal of the Society for Army Historical Research, LXXV, No.302, Summer 1997.

THE PLATES

COLONIAL COMPAGNIES FRANCHES DE LA MARINE 1749-60

A1: Officer The regulation grey-white and blue uniforms worn by the Compagnies franches de la Marine in the French colonies in America were very similar be they in New France, the West Indies or Guyana. There were some attempts to use lighter weight materials in tropical climates, but this seems to have been limited. Officers at full dress parades carried spontoons and swords, wore gorgets and, if senior enough, might have the coveted Cross of St Louis hung on a scarlet ribbon at the breast. Created in 1693 by Louis XIV, the Royal and Military Order of St Louis knighted officers with long and distinguished service careers. Hundreds of colonial officers earned the cross, especially in Canada.

A2: Sergeant NCOs were armed with halberds for formal occasions. Up to 1749, sergeants had gold lace at the cuff buttonholes as a rank badge, but thereafter, this was replaced by edging lace at the cuffs and pocket flaps.

A3: Cadet à l'aiguillette Cadets only existed in Canada, Ile Royale and Louisiana. They were distinguished by a blue and white aiguillette, but otherwise were dressed, armed and equipped as private soldiers.

A4: Drummer The Compagnies franches being royal troops, their musicians wore the king's livery. Until the middle of the 18th century, the drummer's lace was usually set in rows, but thereafter, the fashion of large loops on the breast as shown became prevalent.

A5: Private The corporals and fusiliers were armed with muskets, bayonets and swords and, in the colonies, were equipped with the *gargoussier* belly box and powder horn with its own narrow sling well into the 1750s.
(Reconstructed from numerous documents, especially clothing bills, mostly in the Archives Nationales, Colonies, series B and F1A, and the Rochefort Archives)

CANADIAN MILITIA & AUXILIARIES c.1715-60

B1: Indian Warrior Eastern woodland Indians, especially the Canadian Iroquois and Abenakis, were among the most steadfast allies of the French in Canada. Their villages were often close to the French settlements and they served with the Canadian Militia. Their basic dress and equipment was much the same as the Canadians, but they retained various native decorative features such as war paint.

B2: Officer This officer wears the standard Canadian costume when out in the wilderness. Officers' possessions were often of better quality than average: the cap, for example, might be trimmed with fur. They were distinguished by the gilt gorget. (F. Back & R. Chartrand, 'Canadian Militia 1750-1760', *Military Collector & Historian*, 1984)

B3: Militiaman, cold weather campaign There was practically no season or weather, no matter how hostile, that could stop seasoned Canadian militiamen on campaign in the wilderness. Our figure wears the long capot most suitable in winter, mitts, and other protective items. Snowshoes (not shown) were also essential. (F. Back, 'S'habiller à la Canadienne', *Cap-aux-Diamants*, No. 24, 1991)

B4: Militiamen in summer campaign As surprising as it may sound, the months of July and August can be stiflingly hot and humid in Canada. Canadian militiamen would then often wear only a shirt, breechclouts, mitasses and moccasins. Even sashes and caps might be laid aside.

CANONNIERS-BOMBARDIERS 1750-60

C1: Officers The various companies of this corps of regular colonial artillery all had an identical uniform of blue faced with red. Officers had uniforms of fine quality materials, the red cloth being actually scarlet with silver buttons. Waistcoats could be trimmed with silver lace, and a gilt gorget would be worn on duty.

C2: Gunner This was an élite corps whose men enjoyed higher pay and were to serve as grenadiers, posted at the honoured right of the line at parades, when not serving guns.

C3: Gun crew When serving guns, the men often laid their coats and equipment aside for ease of movement.

French war galley sailing into Marseille in the early 18th century. Until 1748, there was a *Marine des Galères* (galley navy) with all the prerogatives of a distinct navy, and based in Marseille. By the 18th century the rapid war galleys had been outclassed by fast sailing warships, but were useful as coastal patrol ships against Arab raiders. The Galley Navy had its own general, selected from the high nobility, and had several types of troops. (Musée de la ville de Marseille)

C4: Sergeant Sergeants had two silver laces edging the cuffs. (Reconstructed from orders and clothing bills in the Archives Nationales, Colonies, series A, C11B and F1A; R. Chartrand, 'L'artillerie coloniale française, 1534-1791', *Carnet de la Sabretache*, No. 109E, 1991)

CORPS IN CANADA 1750s-60

D1: Trooper, Corps of Cavalry, 1759-1760 The cavalry's uniform was a blue single-breasted coat with red collar and cuffs, possibly with red turnbacks, and apparently with fur caps. Officers were observed in white uniforms, most likely the dress of their respective regiments. The corps was reported well armed and equipped with saddlery. (R. Chartrand & E. Lelièpvre, 'French Corps of Cavalry, Canada, 1759-1760', *Military Collector & Historian*, 1976)

D2: Fusilier, Compagnies franches de la Marine, outposts Soldiers in far-away posts and on campaign in the wilderness were dressed and equipped in a mixture of Canadian and Indian items. The capots were probably grey-white as they were frequently made from uniform coats. The headdress may have often been the military forage cap. Indian-style breechclouts, mitasses and moccasins were worn below the waist. (Philippe Aubert de Gaspé, *Les Anciens Canadiens*, Quebec, 1863; Archives Nationales du Québec, NF25)

D3: Sergeant, Compagnies franches de la Marine Battalion, 1757-1760 In 1757, part of the regular colonial troops were formed into a battalion to serve with the metropolitan army battalions. The battalion had colours and consisted of eight fusilier companies. In early 1760 a second battalion was formed and a company of grenadiers was organised for each battalion. Its men were probably equipped as shown with the cartridge box carried over the shoulder like the metropolitan army. Sergeants on campaign in Canada were equipped with muskets and bayonets like their men.

D4: Militiaman, 'Royal-Syntaxe' Company, 1759 This company was nicknamed 'Royal-Syntaxe' as it was made up of 35 students from the Quebec City Seminary, the institution where higher education could be obtained in Canada. It is now Laval University. The student-militiamen probably wore their school uniform, a blue capot piped white with a white sash and a tricorn. (F. Back, 'Des petits messieurs au capot bleu', *Cap-aux-Diamants*, No. 2, 1988)

D5: Militiaman, Milice de Réserve, 1752-1760 These 'reserve' companies, one in each city of Montreal and Quebec, were ordered formed by Governor-General Duquesne, to consist of wealthy bourgeois merchants led by gentlemen. They wore a scarlet uniform with white cuffs and waistcoat. (Sr. de Courville, 'Mémoire sur le Canada', *Rapport de l'Archiviste de la Province de Québec,* 1924-1925)

AFRICA AND THE INDIAN OCEAN

E1: Fusilier, French East India Company Troops, 1720s-1737. The early dress of these troops in India and Indian Ocean islands was somewhat varied. In the early 1720s, for instance, lemon yellow cloth was slow to sell in the Pondichery trade, so it was made up into uniforms. But thereafter red, which was also used by the Dutch, the Danish and the British troops in India, was worn by the French until 1737. Weapons and equipment were generally as in the army. (Archives Nationales, Colonies, C2, 74; P. Haudrère, *La Compagnie des Indes Française au XVIIIe Siècle*, Paris, 1989, Vol. 3)

E2: Fusilier, French East India Company Troops, c.1750 The Company's infantrymen serving at its base, the port of Lorient in France, in the fort in Senegal and as marines on the Company's ships wore a grey-white uniform faced with blue, almost identical to that of the Compagnies franches de la Marine.

E3: Habitant, Ile de France and Ile de Bourbon Militia, 1740s-1750s The *Habitants* were small farmers and tradesmen of modest incomes who wore inexpensive blue and white check light cloth from India and served as infantry.

RIGHT **Officer, Compagnies franches des Galères, Marseille, c.1718. Grey-white coat, red cuffs, lining, waistcoat, breeches and stockings, gold buttons and lace. The lace edging the coat was worn until about 1730. (Private collection)**

FAR RIGHT **Capitaine d'armes, Compagnies franches des Galères, Marseille, c.1718. Grey-white coat, red cuffs, lining, waistcoat, breeches and stockings, gold buttons, gold hat lace, gold lace at cuffs buttonholes and edging the cuffs and pocket flaps, buff waistbelt. (Private collection)**

E4: Dragoon, Ile de France and Ile de Bourbon Militia, 1740s-1750s The reasonably well-off militiamen who owned a horse were to serve as dragoons and provide themselves with uniform, equipment and arms.

E5: Gendarme, Ile de France and Ile de Bourbon Militia, 1740s-1750s The Gendarmes gathered the wealthiest inhabitants. Their luxurious uniforms were inspired by the gendarmes of the royal guard and were worn well into the 1750s; new hats with gold lace and white plumes were ordered in 1756. This may have been the basis for the red uniforms of the volunteers from the islands who went to India in the *Volontaires de Bourbon*. (Archives de la Réunion, Co 1231 and 1506)

WEST INDIES

F1: Private, de la Roche's Battalion, Martinique, 1761-1762 La Roche de la Touche's was one of the battalions organised in October 1761. It had a 'blue uniform, yellow cuffs and lapels', and the waistcoat and breeches were probably blue. It is also known that Thomasseau's battalion, had a 'blue and white' uniform. (Rufz, *Études historiques et statistiques*...)

F2: Officer with colour, Company of Fusiliers, Du Cap Militia, Haiti, 1740 This company of 50 men plus four Black drummers and fifers was formed on 17 January 1740. Its uniform was: blue coat, red cuffs, collar, waistcoat, breeches and stockings, gold buttonhole lace and buttons, gold-laced hat, red and blue cockade. Its colour was a white cross sprinkled with gold fleurs-de-lis, blue and red quarters. It cost its members over 50,000 pounds to clothe, equip and arm.

(Moreau de Saint-Méry, *Description...de la partie française de l'île de Saint-Domingue*, Philadelphia, 1797)

F3: Fusilier, Karrer's (Swiss) Regiment (Hallwyl's from 1752) c.1740-1763 Uniforms, equipment and weapons for this regiment were procured by the colonel and not supplied by the Navy. They seem to have followed more closely what was used by Swiss units in the metropolitan army. Muskets, for instance, came from St Etienne from the 1720s.

F4: Trooper, Gendarmes of Saint-Pierre, Martinique c.1740-1762 This company wore a light grey-blue coat, red lining, scarlet cuffs, scarlet waistcoat laced with gold, scarlet breeches and stockings, gold buttons and hat lace. (J. Petitjean-Roger, 'La milice de la Martinique au premier siècle de la colonisation', *Revue historique de l'Armée*, 1963)

F5: Trooper, Captain Demassin's Company of Dragoons, Martinique, 1761-1762. In December 1761, this new 'Dragoon company was formed in Saint-Pierre having a blue uniform with pink cuffs and lapels, silver buttonhole lace and aiguillette'. The company was attached to La Roche's battalion. (Rufz, *Études historiques et statistiques*...)

INDIA

G1: Fusilier, 1st French Company, Bussy's Army, 1751-1755 Bussy's force in the Decan had a fantastic array of colourful locally made uniforms. The three French companies had red uniforms and caps faced with green from June 1751 until 1755. In June 1753, distinctive epaulettes were mentioned for each company, the first company having white. (A. Depréaux, 'Les uniformes de l'armée de la Compagnie des Indes d'après un journal inédit de la campagne du Décan

1751-1755', *Revue d'Histoire des Colonies Françaises*, 1926)

G2: Fusilier, European Infantry, French East India Company, c.1737-1750 The uniform of troops posted in India and the Indian Ocean islands was ordered changed from red to blue with red cuffs in 1737. The change must have been made over the next couple of years considering it took six months for a ship to travel from France to India. Company troops adopted the *giberne* style cartridge box, probably over several years, during the 1740s. (Archives Nationales, Colonies, C2, 27 and 81)

G3: Fusilier, Company of Topas, Bussy's Army, 1753-1754 This body of Indo-Portuguese Christians was reported in a pink or buffish pink uniform with red facings. Topas usually spoke Portuguese and were excellent auxiliaries to European troops.

G4: Sepoy, Nellore District, c.1750-1755 The majority of the 10,000 Sepoys in French service wore their Indian-style costume, but some did have European-style uniform jackets in various colours. A Sepoy company in Nellore wore the yellow faced green shown. (A. Depréaux, ed., 'Mémoire sur la Milice des Cipayes au service de la Compagnie des Indes' *Revue d'Histoire des Colonies Françaises*, 1928)

G5: Trooper, Company of Bussy's Guards, 1753-1755 General Bussy had a dozen guards dressed in red faced with green, which were probably the colours of his livery, in a style reminiscent of the royal guards.

NAVAL TROOPS

H1: Fusiliers, Compagnies franches des Galères (galley marines), c.1740 The marines serving on board the Mediterranean fleet of galleys wore basically the same uniform as the sailing ship marines except that their grey-white uniform was faced with red, the traditional colour of the galley fleet, instead of blue. (Lemau de la Jaisse, *Septième Abrégé...*, 1741)

H2: Garde de l'Étendart réal des Galères c.1740 These were naval cadets training to become officers in the galley navy. Usually from noble families in Provence, the youths of the company had a reputation around Marseille for outlandish behaviour. (Lemau de la Jaisse, *Septième Abrégé...*, 1741)

H3: Capitaine d'armes, Compagnies franches de la Marine (ship marines), c.1740 The marines had essentially the same uniform as the colonial troops shown on Plate A, but some details were different. For instance the grey-white cuffs and small standing collar shown are mentioned in the 1740 register. (Lemau de la Jaisse, *Septième Abrégé...*, 1741)

H4: Gunner, Bombardier de la Marine, c.1754 The artillerymen in the three companies of naval artillery were élite troops, specialist in operating mortars in bomb ketches and acting as grenadiers when not serving artillery. They therefore had grenadier caps and sabres. (Painting of the port of Toulon by J. Vernet in the Musée de la Marine, Paris)

Comite in a war galley. Soldiers did not oversee the rowers in galleys as is often believed. This was the job of the *comites* who had to make sure that the galley slaves gave their best efforts. The rowers were supposed to be 'Turks' but most were Frenchmen condemned to the galley for severe crimes. Usually stripped to the waist when rowing, these convicts had their heads shaved and wore red caps with red smocks and trousers. (Print after Maurice Toussaint)

ABOVE **Boarding sabre, c.1750. This type of sabre has been found in several sites in North America as well as in the wreck of the French frigate *Le Machault*, sunk in 1760. The brass half-shell guards were badly cast and were obviously rejected for regular swords. But they could still be used to make cheap boarding sabres. Any old blade and a variety of grips would be quickly assembled with these guards to make crude cutlasses for the Navy, some of which also ended up in New France. (Mr. & Mrs. Don Troiani Collection)**

Notes sur les Planches en Couleur

A Compagnies coloniales franches de la Marine 1749 - 60
A1: Officier. Uniforme réglementaire gris-blanc et bleu que portaient les Compagnies franches de la Marine **A2:** Sergent. Jusqu'en 1749, les sergents avaient un galon doré aux boutonnières des manchettes comme signe de grade, mais il fut remplacé par un galon de bordure **A3:** Cadet à l'aiguillette Les Cadets existaient uniquement au Canada, à l'Ile Royale et en Louisiane.
A4: Tambour. Comme les Compagnies franches étaient des troupes royales, leurs musiciens portaient généralement la livrée du roi. **A5:** Simple soldat. Dans les colonies, en plus d'un mousquet, d'une baïonnette et d'une épée, les caporals portèrent un "gargoussier" et une corne à poudre presque jusqu'en 1760.

B Milice et Auxiliaires canadiens, v. 1715-60
B1: Guerrier indien. Les Iroquois et Abenakis canadiens comptèrent parmi les plus loyaux alliés de la France. **B2:** Officier. Cet officier porte le costume canadien ordinaire durant les expéditions dans la nature. **B3:** Milicien, campagne par temps froid. **B4:** Miliciens en campagne estivale. Habillés pour la chaleur étouffante d'une campagne d'été.

C Cannonniers-Bombardiers 1750-60
C1: Officiers. Les diverses compagnies de ce corps portaient un uniforme identique.
C2: Canonnier. Il s'agissait d'un corps d'élite. **C3:** Equipe de pièce. Les hommes mettaient souvent de côté leur manteau et leur matériel pour être plus à l'aise. **C4:** Sergent.

D Corps au Canada, 1750 à 1760
D1: Soldat de cavalerie, Corps de Cavalerie, 1959-1760 **D2:** Fusilier, Compagnies franches de la Marine, avant-postes. Les soldats des postes éloignés s'habillaient et s'équipaient avec un mélange d'articles canadiens et indiens. **D3:** Sergent, Bataillon des Compagnies franches de la Marine, 1757-1760. Ce bataillon fut formé en 1757 pour servir avec l'armée métropolitaine.
D4: Miliciens, Compagnie "Royal-Syntaxe", 1759. Cette compagnie était composée de 35 étudiants du Séminaire de la ville de Québec **D5:** Miliciens, Milice de Réserve, 1752-1760. Ces compagnies de Montréal et de Québec étaient composées de riches bourgeois et marchands, sous les ordres de gentilshommes.

E L'Afrique et l'Océan Indien
E1: Fusilier, Troupes de la Compagnie des Indes Française, 1720-1737. Le premier uniforme de ces troupes varia, initialement jaune citron puis rouge, comme les troupes hollandaises, danoises et britanniques en Inde. **E2:** Fusilier, Troupes de la Compagnie des Indes Française, vers 1750. Ils portaient un uniforme presque identique à celui des Compagnies franches de la Marine et servaient au port de Lorient en France, au fort du Sénégal et comme fusiliers marins dans les navires de la Compagnie. **E3:** Habitant, Milice de l'Ile de France et de l'Ile de Bourbon, 1740 à 1759. Les "Habitants" étaient de petits fermiers et commerçants qui utilisaient du tissu indien bon marché et servaient dans l'infanterie. **E4:** Dragon, Milice de l'Ile de France et de l'Ile de Bourbon, 1740 à 1759. Ceux qui possédaient un cheval et qui étaient plus aisés servaient dans les dragons et fournissaient leur propre uniforme, matériel et armes **E5:** Gendarme, Milice d'Ile de France et de l'Ile de Bourbon, 1740 à 1759. Il s'agissait des habitants les plus riches, comme l'indique leur uniforme.

F Les Antilles
F1: Simple soldat, Bataillon de la Roche, Martinique, 1761-1762. Le bataillon de La Roche de la Touche fut l'un de ceux qui furent organisés en octobre 1761. **F2:** Officier avec étendard, Compagnie de Fusiliers, Milice Du Cap, Haiti, 1740. Cette compagnie de 50 hommes avec quatre tambours et fifres noirs portait veste bleue, manchettes, col, gilet, pantalon et bas rouges, galon de boutonnière et boutons et coûta à ses membres plus de 50 000 livres pour les uniformes, le matériel et les armes. **F3:** Fusilier, Régiment de Karrer (Suisse) (Régiment de Hallwyl à partir de 1752) vers 1740-1760 Les uniformes, le matériel et les armes furent fournis par le colonel et non pas par la Marine. Ils semblent avoir été proches de ce qu'utilisaient les unités suisses de l'armée métropolitaine. **F4:** Soldat de cavalerie, Gendarmes de Saint-Pierre, Martinique, vers 1740-1762 **F5:** Soldat de cavalerie, Compagnie de Dragons du Capitaine Demassin, Martinique, 1761-1762.

G L'Inde
G1: Fusilier, 1e Compagnie Française, Armée de Bussy, 1751-1755. La force de Bussy dans le Décan possédait une fantastique gamme d'uniformes de fabrication locale, très bigarrés.
G2: Fusilier, Infanterie européenne, Compagnie Française des Indes, vers 1737 - vers 1750. L'uniforme fut modifié sur ordre en 1737. On abandonna le rouge en faveur du bleu avec manchettes rouges. **G3:** Fusilier, Compagnie de Topas, Armée de Bussy, 1753-1754. C'étaient d'excellents auxiliaires pour les troupes européennes. **G4:** Cipaye, District de Nellore, vers 1750-1755. Certains cipayes avaient une veste d'uniforme européen. **G5:** Soldat de Cavalerie, Compagnie des Gardes de Bussy, 1753-1755. Une douzaine de gardes, habillés dans un style qui rappelait les gardes royaux.

H Troupes navales
H1: Fusiliers, Compagnies franches des Galères, vers 1740. Le même uniforme que les fusiliers marins de la flotte à voile, mais avec des parements rouges. **H2:** Garde de l'Etendard réal des Galères, vers 1740. Il s'agissait de cadets de la marine qui suivaient une formation d'officiers dans les Galères. **H3:** Capitaine d'armes, Compagnies franches de la Marine, vers 1740. En gros le même uniforme que les troupes coloniales (Planche A), à certaines exceptions près. **H4:** Canonnier, Bombardier de la Marine, vers 1754. Troupes d'élite spécialisées dans l'utilisation des mortiers dans les ketchs et qui servaient de grenadiers lorsqu'ils ne s'occupaient pas d'artillerie.

Farbtafeln

A Koloniale Compagnies franches de la Marine 1749-60
A1: Offizier. Die vorschriftsmäßigen grauweiß-blauen Uniformen der Compagnies franches de la Marine. **A2:** Feldwebel. Bis 1749 hatten Feldwebel als Rangabzeichen Goldlitzen an den Manschetten-Knopflöchern, danach Randlitzen. **A3:** Cadet à l'aiguillette. Die Kadetten gab es nur in Kanada, der Ile Royale und in Louisiana. **A4:** Trommler. Da die Compagnies franches königliche Truppen waren, trugen ihre Musiker die Livree des Königs. **A5:** Gefreiter. In den Kolonien trugen die Obergefreiten und Füsiliere neben Musketen, Bajonetten und Schwertern bis in die 50er Jahre des 18. Jahrhunderts die "gargoussier"-Bauchtasche und das Pulverhorn.

B Kanadische Miliz & Hilfstruppen, ca. 1715-60
B1: Indianischer Krieger. Die kanadischen Irokesen und Abenakis zählten zu den treuesten Verbündeten der Franzosen. **B2:** Offizier. Dieser Offizier trägt die kanadische Standardkleidung für die Wildnis. **B3:** Milizionär, Kaltwetter-Feldzug. **B4:** Milizionäre auf dem Sommerfeldzug. Bekleidung für den drückend heißen kanadischen Sommer.

C Cannonniers-Bombardiers 1750-60
C1: Offiziere. Die verschiedenen Kompanien dieses Korps trugen alle die gleiche Uniform. **C2:** Schütze. Es handelte sich hierbei um ein Elitekorps. **C3:** Schützenmannschaft. Jacken und Ausrüstung wurden zur Erleichterung der Bewegungsfreiheit oft abgelegt. **C4:** Feldwebel.

D Korps in Kanada, 1750-60
D1: Soldat, Kavalleriekorps, 1759-1760. **D2:** Füsilier, Compagnies franches de la Marine, Vorposten. Bekleidung und Ausrüstung der Soldaten in entlegenen Posten bestand aus einer Mischung kanadischer und indianischer Artikel. **D3:** Feldwebel, Bataillon der Compagnies franches de la Marine, 1757-1760. Das Bataillon wurde 1757 gegründet und diente mit den mutterländischen Heeresbataillonen. **D4:** Milizionär, 'Royal-Syntaxe'-Kompanie, 1759. Diese Kompanie bestand aus 35 Studenten des Seminars der Stadt Quebec **D5:** Milizionär, Milice de Réserve, 1752-1760. Diese Kompanien in Montreal und Quebec setzten sich aus wohlhabenden, bürgerlichen Händlern zusammen und wurden von Edelmännern befehligt.

E Afrika und der Indische Ozean
E1: Füsilier, Truppen der französischen Ostindien-Kompanie, 20er Jahre des 18. Jahrhunderts -1737. Die frühe Bekleidung dieser Truppen war recht unterschiedlich, anfangs zitronengelb danach rot wie der der holländischen, dänischen und britischen Truppen in Indien. **E2:** Füsilier, Truppen der französischen Ostindien-Kompanie, ca. 1750. Die Füsiliere trugen eine Uniform, die mit der der Compagnies franches de la Marine fast identisch war, und dienten im Hafen von Lorient in Frankreich, im Fort in Senegal und als Marineinfanteristen auf den Schiffen der Kompanie. **E3:** Habitant, Miliz der Ile de France und Ile de Bourbon, 40er-50er Jahre des 18. Jahrhunderts. Die Habitants waren Kleinbauern und Händler, die preiswerten Stoff aus Indien trugen und in der Infanterie dienten. **E4:** Dragoner, Miliz der Ile de France und Ile de Bourbon, 40er-50er Jahre des 18. Jahrhunderts. Die relativ wohlhabenden Milizionäre, die ein Pferd besaßen, dienten als Dragoner und kamen für ihre Uniform und Ausrüstung selbst auf. **E5:** Gendarme, Miliz de la France und Ile de Bourbon, 40er-50er Jahre des 18. Jahrhunderts. Sie stammten aus den wohlhabendsten Bevölkerungsschichten, wie aus ihren Uniformen ersichtlich ist.

F Westindische Inseln
F1: Gefreiter, de la Roche-Bataillon, Martinique, 1761-1762. Das Bataillon von La Roche de la Touche war eines der Bataillone, die im Oktober 1761 ausgehoben wurden. **F2:** Offizier mit Fahne, Füsilier-Kompanie, Du Cap-Miliz, Haiti, 1740. Diese 50köpfige Kompanie mit vier schwarzen Trommlern und Pfeifern trug blaue Jacken mit roten Manschetten, Krägen, Westen, Breeches und Strümpfen, goldenen Knopflochlitzen und Goldknöpfen. Die Angehörigen der Kompanie bezahlten über 50.000 Pfund für die Uniform, die Ausrüstung und die Waffen. **F3:** Füsilier, Karrers (schweizerisches) Regiment (ab 1752 Hallwyls), ca. 1740-63. Die Uniformen, die Ausrüstung und die Waffen für dieses Regiment beschaffte der Oberst und nicht die Marine. Sie ähnelten eher der Ausstattung der schweizerischen Einheiten im mutterländischen Heer. **F4:** Soldat, Gendarme von Saint-Pierre, Martinique, ca. 1740-1762. **F5:** Soldat, Captain Demassins Dragoner-Kompanie, Martinique, 1761-1762.

G Indien
G1: Füsilier, 1. französische Kompanie, Bussys Armee, 1751-1755. Bei Bussys Streitkräften im Dekhan sah man eine bestechende Vielfalt vor Ort gefertigter farbenfroher Uniformen.
G2: Füsilier, europäische Infanterie, französische Ostindien-Kompanie, ca. 1737-ca. 1750. Die Uniformen wurden 1737 von rot zu blau mit roten Manschetten geändert. **G3:** Füsilier, Topas-Kompanie, Bussys Heer, 1753-1754. Es waren ausgezeichnete Hilfstruppen für die europäischen Truppen. **G4:** Sepoy, Nellore-Distrikt, ca. 1750-1755. Einige Sepoys trugen Uniformjacken im europäischen Stil. **G5:** Soldat, Kompanie der Bussy-Garde, 1753-1755. Ein Dutzend Gardemitglieder in Uniformen, die an die königliche Garde erinnern.

H Marinetruppen
H1: Füsiliere, Compagnies franches des Galères (Galeeren-Marinetruppen), ca. 1740. Die Marineinfanteristen trugen abgesehen von den roten Aufschlägen im wesentlichen die gleiche Uniform wie die Marineinfanteristen auf den Segelschiffen. **H2:** Garde de l'Étendart réal des Galères, ca. 1740. Marinekadetten bei der Ausbildung zum Offizier in der Galeerenmarine.
H3: Capitaine d'armes, Compagnies franches de la Marine (Marineinfanteristen), ca. 1740. Im wesentlichen dieselbe Uniform wie der der Kolonialtruppen (Tafel A), allerdings mit einigen unterscheidenden Merkmalen. **H4:** Schütze, Bombardier de la Marine, ca. 1754. Elitetruppen bedienen Mörser auf Bombenketschen. Wenn sie nicht bei der Artillerie zum Einsatz kamen, dienten sie als Grenadiere.